In the Absence of Human Beauty

Philosophical Fragments

In the Absence of Human Beauty

Philosophical Fragments

Matthew Alun Ray

BOOKS

Winchester, UK
Washington, USA

First published by iff Books, 2015
iff Books is an imprint of John Hunt Publishing Ltd., Laurel House, Station Approach,
Alresford, Hants, SO24 9JH, UK
office1@jhpbooks.net
www.johnhuntpublishing.com
www.iff-books.com

For distributor details and how to order please visit the 'Ordering' section on our website.

Text copyright: Matthew Alun Ray 2014
Library of Congress Control Number: 2015936390

ISBN: 978 1 78279 927 6

A CIP catalogue record for this book is available from the British Library.

Design: Lee Nash

Printed in the USA by Edwards Brothers Malloy

We operate a distinctive and ethical publishing philosophy in all
areas of our business, from our global network of authors to
production and worldwide distribution.

To my Mother

Acknowledgements

First of all, I must first discharge three personally and academically vital debts: to Stephen Cheeke, Devorah Baum and Antonio Gomez, all of whom are friends who read significant portions of the present work in a more primeval form. I cannot shift all of the responsibility for any mistakes or errors onto them (though our friendships could easily bear the strain of that). I have also benefited personally and greatly from help from, and I am also more generally indebted to, my mother – to whom the book is dedicated, now more than ever – and my father, Gemma, Nico and Dave, Adrian Williams, Dr. Henry Morriss, Craig Holden, Suzy and Tommy Cheeke, Mark Evans and Paul Evans, Gwyn Topham, Joanna Brown, Bernadette Thomas, Josh Appignanesi, Dr Jenny Dundrow, Angela Baum, Bethan Stevens, Anton Goldenstein, Chris Ozzard, Bishop Emeritus Mullins, Rabbi Yehoshua Engelman and Maria Villa Escallon. I have also profited immensely from the encouragement offered to previous versions of this project from Anthony Rudd, Caroline Wilde and Birna Birnadottir.

He who wants to hold fragments of this kind to their promise may be an honourable man – only he is not to pretend to be a poet. Must one always be deliberate?

– Novalis, *Miscellaneous Observations* § 120

– It is not that our search for satisfaction has its limits, but that satisfaction is *itself* a limit.

– The face is the one thing that cannot be incorporated into a fetish.

– The souls of the dead grieve for their bodies, temporarily.

– We fail to know the Other. I wonder what success would mean?

– Poetry cannot be entered from the outside.

– Where should the Other find any sympathy if not in *you*? You are irreplaceable – "appointed" or "elect" in the vocabulary of one recent philosopher – in at least this sense. You cannot delegate *this* responsibility.

– That which is *now* no longer exists. It never did.

– One of Jean-Paul Sartre's more arresting passages in *L'Être et le néant: Essai d'ontologie phénoménologique* most meticulously describes a solitary walk through the park. In our little journey without purpose, we take in the damp grass, the soggy municipal bench, and then, with a psychological (and perhaps even an ethical) jolt, we immediately become aware of the presence of another person in the park; the park we had hitherto felt or imagined to be wholly deserted. What we (or, at least, what some) can tend to think of as our default *epistemological* position is shattered and we are momentarily unsettled; we realize instantly that we are co-visible: suddenly, we are awkwardly aware of what Sartre technically terms a 'secondary centre of reference'. We become cognizant of another point of view specifically on what we see: the grass and the park bench on a steep, uninhabited hill are acknowledged by the *other* but we know that they are acknowledged by this particular other in a different way from the way that *we* grasp them; they are organized (or apprehended, or synthesized, or are being seen) quite differently by, or from, his or her standpoint, and we now have to take this standpoint explicitly into account: both into an ontological account of the world as well as into moral account. The world – as is the case in Heidegger's *Being and Time* – is now grasped as 'mine too'. Taken to its most extreme, such a simple epistemological acknowledgment of an *other* can lead to a diversion of psychic energies from their normal and typically egotistic functioning and a self-destructive attachment – a *cathexis* is the psychoanalytic term, a *crystallization* is the metaphorically botryoidal term invented by Stendhal in *De L'Amour* – to this other. This moment of diverting libidinal energy directly to the other and away from the self highlights an unhealthy diminution of our feelings of power and self-worth, a poverty of confidence in the quest for self-preservation that finds its ultimate limit in the outer shores of abandonment; an abandonment that we – with some justification – call love.

– Religion and existentialism perhaps converge in the following proposition: *one must concentrate on the purity of the act.*

– It's obvious at first glance that the phenomenon which checks my vision is frequently only vision once again; the vision of another subject with a vision of his own. The face – the ineffaceable but still ineffable fact of bodily expression – is the sight of subjectivity.

– The battle of the wills is worked out on the plane of the gaze.

– *Both husband and wife appear to the observer together. Harry, inside the town house, walking around, is wearing a linen bathrobe, or dressing gown. His hair is wet, though not actually sopping. He is newly shaved and has possibly even missed a bit, under the chin. Phillipa is just entering the house through the front door and has had an evening out, attending, as it happens, a lecture on the measures necessary for the ecological protection of the future of the planet. ("Fascinating stuff" Harry had commented, earlier that day.) Phillipa is, externally, wearing a stylish trench coat with a check lining and is, internally, emotionally electrified: "What a sensational speaker." "Who?" "Alexander Feuchtwanger, of course." "Oh." "You know who I mean?" "Never heard of him." "You're sure you haven't heard of him?" "He hasn't come to my attention." "How was your evening?" "My evening?" " How was your bath?" "One of the best." "Sorry?" "It was literally one of the best baths that I have ever had." "One of the best baths you have ever had? "Yes, that's more or less what I said."*

– *She turns away from her husband and looks toward the long hall mirror, initially to glance at the state of her own hair but, for a second, she looks into the mirrored, living green of her own eyes and continues speaking. In the mirror (within its limits), Harry is out of sight. Yet he is still listening attentively to every single word that she utters. He wouldn't want to come between her and her precious emotions.*

– In some of his most exploratory philosophical fragments, Wittgenstein gave an articulate voice to the notion that the solipsist could not, in principle, achieve the ability to think privately and, as a consequence of his inability, couldn't even advance his own opinion: that is, he couldn't even articulate his own philosophical position; for, of course (of course?), thinking itself uses words – and how would a single individual, metaphysically entirely on his own, be able to really *know* that he was using words acceptably? This (at least, apparent) indiscriminate dismissal of a certain privacy of thought can be set side by side both with Søren Kierkegaard's theological claim that God does not think and with Kant's original idea that God's mode of being is 'intellectual intuition', a manner which does not use or involve discursive – hence linguistic – thought. (The Kantian and post-Kantian identification of God's thought with His creation remains constant to the traditional doctrine of Divine *simplicity*.) It might be urged here that God is omniscient, anyway – so this whole human idea of following rules has no application to Him, save an analogous or metaphoric one – still, might this omniscience be rendered more humanly understandable by figuring it as a mode of creating rather than thinking? Is this even intelligible? Is the point that it should not be? – But didn't God create man in God's own image? – Yet aren't we prohibited from the creation of idols?

– *"Yes, it is unquestionable that medieval debates over the **naming** of God and the unknowing associated with Him and his Infinity have resurfaced in recent debates over the Other." Phillipa claimed. Harry added: "Perhaps the time has come for us to envision a new religion, a religion without language." Phillipa chastened him with one of her dismissive looks. "Do you want us to all troop down to Mass and sit there in silence?" said the man in the purple jacket.*

– Surprisingly, the concept of a *pilgrimage* still appears to be a potent one. It has certainly long since outstripped its purely religious usage. Such a cultural shift is typified by the examples of two different, over-excitable people that I have recently overheard. Both were referring, on separate occasions, to a personal "pilgrimage" they'd made *to the Galapagos Islands*! (Why not Westminster Abbey, where Darwin is, in any case, buried?) Such a crypto-religious account of their scientific travels would have displeased Nietzsche, who pinpointed the "search for truth" as the last refuge of the religious "ascetic ideal". In these contemporary "scientific" "pilgrimages", the traveller seems to have somewhat naively separated the power of the scientific discoverer from the nature of the scientific discovery itself, unless such pilgrims are (highly improbable though it might seem) attempting an arch reference to a sinister religious pilgrimage to the heart of nihilism itself, a black ritual to honour the competition that grinds out the breeds.

– We immediately assign reality a subject of experience, – "I". *Our* eyes, *our* fields of vision, *our* bodies: these are frequently to be found at the dead centre of the real, as a dimension of manifestation. (One thinks of the basic structure of philosophical investigation in modernity from Descartes through empiricism to Husserlian phenomenology.) I already say "our" rather than "mine" because it is intuitively natural to then go on to accept the proposal that reality embraces the existence of others. (The *Daseinanalytik* embraces *Mitsein* without fanfare.) Others surround us but they are usually explicitly noted only – a point that Levinas, above all others, has driven home – insofar as they incommode us. (Like broken implements: they are in need.) But the leap from the abstract acceptance of others to *fully keeping in mind* that the Other does not revolve around us but actually possesses a full subjectivity, too (that is, the leap to our sense that he occupies a point that is of no essential ontological or ethical difference to ours) is an ongoing practical process of learning a certain moral truth. (And how long does learning to take on board a moral truth take?)

– To raise the faces of others out of the anonymous buzz that is presented to our senses, one must be able to afford to allow or grant an *expressive* tendency to certain representations; which is, in itself, a partly moral affirmation in the guise of a purely epistemological one. One must *acknowledge* or *read* the expressive tendencies of the Other. The *morally-existentially foundational* element of the intersubjective encounter is evident, to give but one example, in *Totality and Infinity* by E. Levinas, who straightforwardly declares that: 'To recognize an other is to recognize a hunger'[1]. This admission that others seem to be acknowledged only insofar as they trouble us couldn't be made in starker terms. To raise faces out of the mere murmur of data, it is enough to assume a certain responsibility for helping them in their need (which, it is at least tacitly admitted, as expressed is already embodied); to pity them – as Wittgenstein once said – already being a conviction. More generally, one could say that the other appears only insofar as it makes such a *moral appeal*. Levinas does not hesitate to say this, accordingly introducing the splicing of his position with a metaphysics of expression (a metaphysics that will not generate any criticism from the present author). He does so, for example, in the following citation: 'Expression manifests the presence of being, but not simply by drawing aside the veil of the phenomenon. It is of itself the presence of a face and hence appeal.'[2] Hunger; appeal; Otherness.

– Flesh is the very fabric of human expression. And expression does not *externalize* the purportedly wholly "inner self" as much as constitute it. *As a matter of fact, nothing is hidden.* The enigmatic Wittgensteinian space between the Other and myself is the very space of expression. It appears to have been Schopenhauerian expressivism that gave Wittgenstein a superior explanation for the unity of mind and body that mainstream modern philosophy, after Descartes, had been spectacularly unable to provide (since that particular philosophy had, by its very adoption of a mind/body categorization, driven a wedge between the inner and the outer human being). The only path out of this philosophical impasse intrinsic to ontological dualism is to retrace one's steps, abandon the mainstream division of mind and body and to embrace instead a (forgotten, or neglected, perhaps a Schopenhauerian) non-causal expressivist account of the body as an *expression* or manifestation of *the willing self* and certainly not of the inner, detached 'mind' – a category that was idealistically privileged not only by Descartes (but when seen through Schopenhauer's eyes is nothing but a mere instrument).

– I catch sight of the Other without being able to pinpoint her essence in the exact features of her face. She shimmers under, glints in or hovers over her face. This experience – this epiphany – is to be taken as point of departure. Our acknowledgement of the Other (prompted and located by the flicker of expression), our address to them, certainly our sympathy for them, isn't impeded by their otherness.

– It cannot be seen – so it must be read.

– The Other is the permanent reality of expression, until the terrible day when his face acquires an unprecedented solidity.

– One way to attempt a straightforward explanation of expression would set off as follows: it isn't that her happiness is located *in there somewhere* behind the smile: in the skull beneath a face that offers us a symptom of it (in a secret system of life in which thoughts and feelings circulate in a cold vaccum of abstraction and inspection). No: our vibrant emotions, in line with all other feelings to a greater or a lesser degree, are ventilated in – that is simply to say, expressed through – our beaming faces. *There is nothing essential to the subject sealed deep within the tissue that cannot, in principle, be expressed in and upon the countenance and the flesh.* A flickering uncertainty of the features *is* an uncertainty (of the "mind"). Similarly, our uneasy grimaces are a very part of our being troubled – not mere superficial masks that may or may not fail to cover it. Countless other examples will bring us to the same conclusion. We can, for example, invoke conclusions found in the phenomenology of Max Scheler here, in addition to the insights of Schopenhauer, Levinas, Cavell and Wittgenstein, amongst others. We can even move further afield – to zoosemiotics, for example – so as to reinforce this point. For, leaving our own species (just for a moment), we might point out that the dog's wagging tail and his fawning, devoted demeanour toward his master is as about as expressive of the feelings of a being as one could possibly imagine (a point about canine expression that had not gone unnoticed by either Schopenhauer or Max Scheler). Real contact between human beings – and even between humans and dogs – appears, therefore, to occur *in* the gaze – and there isn't much that is more obvious than that we do make eye contact with dogs – and *on* the trembling flesh and *in* that wagging tail. The "real" being isn't as isolated and anonymous as we would sometimes like to believe.

– That we recognise what is being expressed in the wagging of a dog's tail effectively disposes of the theory that understanding expression involves imitating it. Expressive phenomena *already* provide access to the *life of others*, without invoking further excitement involving a whole slew of concepts such as projection, mimicry etc.

– We must be awake to an acceptance of our body, to both its limits and its highly revealing capacities. This is an acceptance that cannot, in any case, be relinquished upon this Earth. (Except, perhaps, in the deepest of sleeps.)

– Levinas notes somewhere (I am unfortunately unable to relocate the reference) that: "To sleep is to suspend physical and psychic activity." I might immediately add that there does exist an explicit thesis to the contrary: "There is no such thing as sleep" – this was the bewitching thesis of Devorah Baum and if it departs from the 'sleep-as-suspension' proposal in its intuitive sensing of the impossible possession of outright psychic respite, it nevertheless coheres both with the empirical fact that Rationalism enters into philosophy only by means of a dream and that Empiricism exits philosophy, by contrast, by means of every dream that has ever presented us with clear and vivid impressions.

– The stream of consciousness has interruptions. The body has replacements.

– One might ask, taking up certain strands of Descartes' narrative from the *Meditationes de prima philosophia*, whether it is possible to dream from the subjective viewpoint of another? Such a bizarre question as this appears to be unobjectionably answered in the negative by Ludwig Feuerbach: 'It is the same ego, the same being, in dreaming as in waking'.[3] Yet perhaps what Feuerbach – whose pointedly unCartesian interest was, he claimed, in real *embodied men* and not with *abstractions such as the ego* – perhaps fails to add here is that it is *not the same body* in sleep as that body which is (represented? felt?) in the life of the dream. There is one body in bed and quite another in the neon circus of our dreamscape.

– There is one body in bed and quite another in the dream space. This may be part of the reason why most major thinkers – with a few notable exceptions, such as Schopenhauer and Freud – have followed Descartes into believing that we are not at all home in the world of the dream.

– We incur responsibilities to the Other simply by being always embedded in what are – in what cannot fail to be – moral situations, situations from which we cannot – without repercussions that are themselves ethical by default (sins of omission) – detach or abstract ourselves. Other people – by their lived existence in propinquity to us, absent any special (or any general) activity on their part – appeal for some kind of a response from us and by repudiating conversation with them – blanking them – completely we are, whether we are explicitly aware of it or not, shirking something; shunning someone. Ethics is responsiveness. We can neither outwait the other nor *excuse ourselves* – nor be literally academically uninvolved – from the imprescriptible exigencies of even the most temperamentally unobtrusive other. The ethical exigency requires avowing rather than avoiding, *or it requires prolonging* such an avowal, such an acknowledgement.

– In refusing or abruptly stopping conversation with an Other, either by physical avoidance or by engaging a third person in a separate, second 'exit conversation', we are "quitting": refusing to engage, ethically absconding. Remember that something as thin as the human eyelid, that something as tender as the muscle in a neck, can wipe the Other from our view. Total abstraction from the personally committed immediacy of such a scenario isn't, as may be initially thought, a neutral philosophical withdrawal from it so as to ponder the very relations of abstractions – unless we count withdrawal from immediacy as itself a *response* that is itself *slighting* to the Other (at least in this inter-subjective context), a deliberate exposure to the blizzard of indifference, the true face of human blankness. Hence Levinas writes with perfect clarity (once again in *Totality and Infinity*) that: 'I have access to the alterity of the Other from the society I maintain with him, and not by quitting this relation in order to reflect on its terms.'[4] If we accept such a straightforward thesis of immediate access articulated here by Levinas then what gives urgency to the epistemological problematic is simply that episte-mological ignorance can be equated with ethical avoidance. It appears that the other's privacy (Wittgenstein) or his silence (Kierkegaard) or his solitude (Nietzsche) or his ineffable Otherness (Levinas) – all of these terms generalize into transcen-dence – somehow makes an appeal on us to do something and by making an *ethically indeclinable* appeal on us at all, he therefore demands immediate recognition – or gets shunned, avoided, ostracized – and thus makes us 'responsible' (in one way – or another) or – according to a different but not entirely unrelated philosophical dispensation – 'sympathetic'. (Referring to Levinas, Schopenhauer and Cavell in the same breath here should remind us that the concepts of embodiment and expression have long been used to serve to elucidate theories of empathy and, more narrowly, sympathy and acknowledgement. Related ideas can also be found in Wittgenstein's writing.)

– There is an imprescriptible exigency enshrined in the face. But the swell of sympathy for Others comes from – and despite itself remains – *inside us*.

– Since its inception in the work of Hegel, if that sub-discipline of philosophical methodology known as phenomenology is to be routinely stigmatised as the programmatic denial of (an alienated) exteriority (or, at least, the stage by stage recapturing and re-assimilation of that exteriority), Levinas could be taken to have precariously accommodated the phenomenological method to a sense of the Outside: that is, to an exteriority without mediation. But the specifically Levinasian accommodation with *the Outside*, one may feel, is not simply a precarious settlement but is actually *a mostly cosmetic one*, since to the extent that Levinas appears to embrace alterity, his writing – howsoever phenomenologically motivated– peels away from its residual methodological bias toward the phenomenological, leading to obvious questions regarding Levinasian thought such as the following: is there really *an experience* of the Other?

– Certain lines of strictly individualist philosophical investigation – empiricism or sentimentalism or phenomenology, for example – are inherently "self-centred". How, then, do we get from such an *individual* encapsulated epistemological viewpoint as this over to the *universal* truth? How do we open ourselves up? Does mystical experience remain an option? Or may obeisance paid to an impartial spectator open us up to the outside, even though that spectator is himself fictional though nonetheless geared toward combating, precisely, selfishness? Aren't there dangers to this form of projection?

– There is a certain telling inevitability to the illusion of the man in the white shirt endlessly falling: like a bone fractured in advance of the fall.

– Regina Olsen stands stock still, her eyes staring out of the window, silent, her clothes partially sunlit and her face strangely beautiful. 'We become what we remember', Plotinus counselled. (Or, as Gustave Flaubert might have said: she has her love story, like everyone else.) It remains true that, for good or for ill, we all display traces of the others who have passed through our lives, like secrets we have been forbidden to keep.

– Philosophical commentators predictably note that Kierkegaard's invocation of inexpressive silence in *Fear and Trembling* – there are other kinds of silence – may be trying to tell Regina Olsen something. – Inwardness and concupiscence. All this to repulse Regina? Lessening her love for him in an act so betraying of and yet so dependent upon love that it is at once infinitely forgivable and yet bereft of any standard of expiation.

– We must imagine Søren Kierkegaard indoors, uttering her name in solitude.

– When Kierkegaard called his book *Fear and Trembling* he referred, in the first word of the title, to an "inner" emotion hidden from everybody (this is the element of private interiority and subjectivity that Kierkegaard was always so attached to) and, in the last word, to an eminently accessible, visibly expressive piece of behaviour. But is all you can see in trembling an indecipherable shaking? Or, rather, especially given, in addition, the contextual cues, don't you perceive something physical that is already *soaked with the meaningful*? Aren't you, in fact, seeing the fear itself? You are surely not involved in a process of inferring it. The meaning does not need to be inferred when the body is imbued with it.

– Will a "knowing smile" tell me that the Other knows something? Answer: Yes.

– When he collapses with grief, his grief is already here in the room (right here in his expressions and in his vocalisations) and is most certainly not ensconced away at the heart of the inner. You almost immediately console him, as best you can. Pity, Wittgenstein wrote, is a form of conviction.

– We enter, as inexorably as fate, into the tedium of *completion* – the silence maintained by the pitiful dead.

– The *Daseinanalytik* of Heidegger's *Being and Time* (Division One) has a core project that may be succinctly characterized as wanting to provide its readers with an extensive sketch of 'ways of being': that is to say, possible ways for *Dasein* to be. (Such 'ways of being' belonging to what I provocatively call here *the subject* are obviously to be rigorously distinguished from the philosophical 'categories' that have comprehensively applied to *objects*, or to what we can *say* about objects, from Aristotle's *Categories* through Kant's *Critique of Pure Reason* and beyond.) From section 45 of *Being and Time* onwards, however, it becomes increasingly clear to the reader that one of these 'ways of being' sketched by Heidegger enjoys a certain prestige over all of the rest: our particular way of *existing-towards-death* or *Sein zum Tode*. Heidegger's appropriation and acknowledgement of grim psychological mortality notably treats death as a *possibility* and not a *biological fact* but it is a matter of possibility that is nevertheless obscured or obliterated in our half awake immersion in "diversions" (in the sense given to that term by Pascal). In what Heidegger, as a consequence, calls our "inauthenticity", have we *forgotten*, therefore, that we are mortal? Have we forgotten our position in the fourfold?

– The most authentic *way of being* for *Dasein* is, it would seem, though Heidegger never quite admitted as much, one who is terminally ill and has been forced to acknowledge this condition of *being-towards-death* where death is accepted – *or deliberately and pointedly rejected* – as a permanent horizon of existential choice.

– For the terminal Heideggerean, aureoled by the majesty of death, each decision now automatically becomes authentic. It is to the terminal Heideggerean that the words *"deliberately and pointedly rejected"* will mean most and so I address and dedicate these words to him, or her.

– The instant of my death, a death amid words, is the loss of possibility (the loss of death *as* a possibility) and, hence, inauthentic.

– *Dasein* doesn't accept death by letting go of life but by grasping life with a stronger will and doing so in full view of death, in the rasping gaze of her non-knowledge. The supposed result is that death irradiates black majesty.

– If con-specificity and social co-presence is necessary for the guarantee of individual ethical correctness (as is suggested by philosophers as disparate as Feuerbach, Wittgenstein, Hutcheson and Adam Smith, as well as many others), then isn't *"the they"*, which was supposedly a mark of Heideggeran inauthenticity, either a mark of confidence in moral authenticity or, alternatively, and as seems more likely, a ruling out of a Heideggerean ethics altogether?

– Death in the concrete is easier to fight than death in the abstract.

– *"Must everything we do be mortgaged to the dead horizon? Death is not a magnet for every act." "And Death Resumes his Dominion." "Every little act in a deathly context? I don't think so, Harry. Examining death is not exactly living." "Well, we will have to agree to disagee on that." "No, you will have to agree with me on that."*

– The anticipative destiny of phenomenological death, a demise typically refused any sacerdotal context whatsoever by Heidegger is far easier to combat existentially than 'death in the abstract', the cold thought that strikes you at nighttime: death from above. Even so, Heideggeran *Sorge* or *care* – I think here of its etymological association with the pastoral term "curate" who looks after the souls of others – is, perhaps, an oblique antidote to the death-cult of *being-towards-death*. (I recall that Levinas occasionally speaks of Heideggeran *Sorge* in terms of a will to live.) Heidegger may indeed attempt to fuse these two ideas but death – it seems to me – bleeds through the fingers of care, which is the very structure of life itself.

– The substance of the Schopenhauerian metaphysics as a considered system – where the body, felt from the inside, is an unexpected naked opening to the senseless, aimless, incomprehensible and amoral will – does not contain anywhere within itself the conceptual resources necessary for understanding or even allowing true goodness. (The *wille* essentially occupies the post where Freud will eventually station the unconscious.) As should be clear, Schopenhauer's philosophy admits only a glum, austere ontology of the *Wille* where, despite what Schopenhauer himself concedes, not a single act of goodness survives or is, in principle, capable of surviving. It is, therefore, an obvious fact that the selfish *Wille* as the ground of Being must be torn away from its identification with the Kantian Thing-in-Itself if there is to be any ontological possibility left for real goodness at all. Goodness is only a fiction if the *Wille* is *exclusively* real. There are essentially two ways of understanding, and thus responding to, this somewhat incommodious philosophical predicament. The first approach involves biting the bullet and admitting there is *no goodness in this world*. Nietzsche comes closest to aligning himself with this amoral trajectory. The second approach is that of viewing the issue in accordance with a set of larger *religious* preoccupations. Schopenhauer himself but also Levinas (who adopts a remarkably similarly basic ontology of selfishness to Schopenhauer) take the second approach: that is to say, both Levinas and Schopenhauer are prompted by their ontology to *mystify goodness*. More specifically, they both outsource the generation of goodness to a process of *grace* i.e. to an *ontological enigma*. (I do not say that they are thereby guilty of an error.) It is worthy of note that the Schopenhauerian-Levinasian theory of grace does *seem* to shift the problem out of ontology altogether. (Where would one search for the origin of grace?) Grace, as this point may also be put, resists a summary analysis. And it would lead us too far afield here to do any more than merely gesture toward a corresponding development – here made in accordance with a vaguely Buddhist rather than monotheistic tenor – within late Heidegger's thought ('*Gelessanheit*') when conciliating a somewhat comparable clash of two opposing notions (i.e. in fostering the notion of being able to will non-willing). But for Schopenhauer, who also, incidentally, had certain Buddhist leanings but who did not, by any means, want to explicitly move beyond metaphysics (though his words themselves are, very infrequently, open to such a reading), it is hardly strange that the presence of such a paradox in his thought suggests that a radical overhaul and transformation of Schopenhauer's metaphysics itself might, in fact, be necessary if that metaphysics is both to allow for goodness and is not to devolve into internal antinomian conflicts. (Schopenhauer was not required by his philosophy to *individually* winkle out God, personal souls and other beings from the realm of the thing-in-itself one by one, since his fusion of Lockean and Kantian ideas made his ontology monistic from the outset. But the internal logic of his overall philosophical progression towards grace regresses effortlessly towards the religious.) Or is it, in fact, possible to somehow reconstruct the moral search for goodness on a foundation other than that of ontology?

– If altruism in our everyday lives is to be taken as *real* then Schopenhauerian *grace* must be taken to be much more than, say, a 'regulative idea' of the Kantian type. So that when Schopenhauer invokes the notion of religious grace to overcome otherwise irresolvable problems in his disarmingly askew metaphysical and ethical philosophy, it is precisely here, at *the second lip of the abyss* (and there is nothing here that takes us far beyond the role played by Levinas' idea of 'sanctity'), more than anywhere else in his system, that Schopenhauer trembles on the brink of a *theological epiphany* – but, admittedly, Schopenhauer stops *far* short of such a revelation. God is just over the horizon for Schopenhauer. But that horizon is transcendental.

– The Levinasian Other *edges* into vectors of our phenomenological periphery: until his true epiphany – typically described in terms that resemble a partially de-transcendentalised Beatific Vision – whereby the finite has absorbed some of the mysteries of the infinite. Yet, ultimately, this vision is, according to Levinas, only ever an oddly partial one: Levinas makes of the face itself almost an afterimage, a mere hint; and makes of expression almost a mere trace. *Is* there really an experience of the Other?

– In the unilateral, asymmetrical relationship that intersubjectively obtains between the other and I, it is always he or she and not I who commands. He commands responsibility. The relationship between subjects is curved, asymmetrical, in this sense. Levinas had a specific term for this kind of uncompromisingly unilateral moral authority, structure or imbalance: 'height'. In intersubjective space, distance is inflected into height. Height, in the sense that Levinas understands it, is always exclusively in his or her hands (most certainly not in ours). Before the Other, we are mere apology, justification through works which imply faith. At this point, it may be that a brief historical flashback so as to introduce a further conceptual element into consideration would be useful. The 'Impartial Spectator', introduced by Adam Smith, can also be read as an Other, but an Other as a *rectifier* – thus figuring a return of others so as to limit the possibility of the capricious judgment of the self, which is an inherent possibility of sentimentalist ethical philosophies. (Moral Knowing as first person *plural*.) Hence, if moral judgment does require an Other, this may be a response to their need and appeal in order to recalibrate and underwrite the intersubjective validity of our – otherwise, at least *potentially* capricious or whimsical – moral judgments. (One thinks also of the precise role of conspecifics in both the epistemology and the moral philosophy of Feuerbach.)

– Irrespective of one's initial thoughts, the figure of the Ideal Observer, the 'Impartial Spectator', quite obviously cannot *himself* lead to the establishment of any substantial epistemological – i.e. contra-sceptical theoretical – link from the self to an other because on reflection such a generic spectator himself can be seen to be *already* standing proxy for and schematising this Other, or this community of others. Nor would someone such as Levinas himself accept this – or any other – form of the impersonal. (I suspect that Levinas would see Cavell's dependence upon ordinary language (and the community of language users), for example, as strictly analogous in this respect to Hegel's references to the universal.) The scepticism that still weighs on Levinas is, therefore, the scepticism of existentialism as such in all its arbitrariness and separation.

– *Harry stands in the long, golden light of the narrow garden, looking, with an understandable degree of fascinated distraction, down at the ground. Phillipa brings him out a cup of tea. "Everything ok?" "Death threatens our companions, the ants." – "You made me a promise, Harry." "In the past I did, yes!" Phillipa smiles: the ants! Things are back to normal.*

– *Two Cheers for Crude Anthropomorphism*: A frenetic army of ruinous ants lay siege; they unflinchingly take their prisoners and transport them as chattels: wreaking furious carnage, slaughter on an immense scale. But have we really any 'proper' scale? Are we failing to detect an Achilles of the ants?

– A demand for *acknowledgement* (I owe the strictly technical use of this term, in the context of obviating scepticism, to Stanley Cavell) is a consequence of any exposure to the expression of the Other. After the philosophical accomplishments of not only Cavell but also Wittgenstein, Schopenhauer and Levinas (as well as many others), it is no longer remotely plausible to construe our acceptance of the supposedly purely "inner" world or "inner" life of the Other as being wholly the ultimate result of an inference. The life (that "inner" life) of the other is an outer expression to be acknowledged (so not exactly a purely "inner" world at all), a simple recognition of the very isthmus of animal expression. Expression is the dynamic structure that links the philosophical "thing-in-itself" to the experienced reality of the visible person in his manifestation. Perhaps the most impressive development *in extenso* of this concept of expression amogst the *writers* listed above, at least in its metaphysical and epistemological usage belongs – somewhat surprisingly – to Schopenhauer. It is in the writings of Schopenhauer, the earliest of these thinkers of expression, that an exposure to the true expression of the Other first represents a pre-emptive anti-sceptical interruption. There thus resides, at least for Schopenhauer, Cavell and Levinas (and quite possibly for Wittgenstein, also), *in the very experience* of the Other's expression, a latent *moral obligation* to respond – the absolute exigency – *the moral impossibility of not responding.*

– What we take to be, say, a passing smile – something we might *primae facie* tend to think of as something superficial – often solidifies not only a communication from *but also an actual contact with* the deep Noumenon. (A broad Kantianism is simply accepted as a frame of philosophical analysis for this thought.) Emotions stand before us in a recognisible enough form.

– The form of our representation might be regarded as being misleading. (The Kantian examples here would be: *space* and *time*.) But not so its *content*. Believe it or not, life is stirring in human beings.

– That we entirely express or wholly manifest ourselves as *will* when we act, without any imperceptible and unapproachable subject-residuum left over, is a thesis set forth without hesitation in a variety of places in Schopenhauer's *The World as Will and Representation*. Allow me to cite just one case in point. Schopenhauer summarily announces, for example, that: 'The act of will and the action of the body are not two different states objectively known, connected by the bond of causality; they do not stand in the relation of cause and effect, but are one and the same thing'[5]. (One can hardly deny that there is a – scarcely coincidental – resemblance here to certain thoughts that are later found in Wittgenstein. One of Wittgenstein's key ways of eluding scepticism is, in truth, obtained by what appears to be merely the limited rehabilitation of Schopenhauer's doctrine of expressivism.) One could easily multiply references to such passages in Schopenhauer. So much, then, for the utter isolation of the purely "inner" life: that life of an occult subjectivity is from now on to be conceived of, in those who have learned from Schopenhauer, as the very same thing as the "outer" life of the body. (Ontologically, it may also be said that Schopenhauer, as has been sufficiently proved by many of his commentators, reduces all phenomena to the metaphysical will, so that his very *monism* in this respect supports the notion of an ultimately reductive view of *mental* processes that would otherwise potentially stymie his outflanking of scepticism by reference to the expressed will.) It is still, of course, theoretically possible (this seems to be the case in Levinas, for example) to be an ontological expressivist and yet to hold that bodily expression, although a no doubt crucial disclosure of the Other, is still *not* a *complete* one, i.e. that expression is, after all, not *absolutely identical* with the observable 'action of the body'. Even so, I believe that Levinas is an exception here and that the dominant philosophical position in the analysis of the concept of human expression, from Schopenhauer through Wittgenstein and on to Stanley Cavell, has been conducted on the assumption – quite alien, I repeat, to Levinas – that we are *wholly given* the Other *in* his bodily expression, so that to exhaustively know an other is, actually, to accurately read an other body. (Of course, we can misread it, too. This is the simian limitation: ability does not entail any infallibility.)

– One of the more notable contributions of the work of, in particular, Stanley Cavell to the philosophical debate on human expression as a tool against scepticism consists in his frequent and unflinching thinking of expression right through human transcendence altogether. Cavell shares a perfectly Schopenhauerian understanding of 'expression' as being exhaustively expressive of the Other (in, for example, his monumental text, *The Claim of Reason*). Such a standpoint, whether in its Schopenhauerian or its Cavellian modulation, resourcefully fuses two hoary philosophical problems (Other-scepticism and Cartesian mind-body interaction) into one basic philosophical issue with a single ontological solution. (The historical assumption here is that raising Other-scepticism is not only a mistake, it is a specifically post-Cartesian mistake. Hence Schopenhauer, like Nietzsche or Rorty or Heidegger, can, therefore, pinpoint with a degree of historical accuracy *the moment when philosophy went awry*.) – By means of contrasting the thought of Levinas with this dominant position of *exhaustive expression* (found from Schopenhauer through Wittgenstein to Cavell), let me now draw out and circumscribe the vagaries of this somewhat different Levinasian position (with at least one degree more clarity). For although Levinas does depend upon the concept of expression to do importantly anti-Cartesian work in his philosophy, the concept of expression itself is cast in a different manner by Levinas from the way it was cast in Schopenhauer (and Cavell), because whereas expression functions in the, broadly speaking, neo-Schopenhauerian tradition in such a manner as to be both ontologically vital and epistemologically exhaustive; in Levinas, on the other hand, the undoubted metaphysical importance of expression in signalling the Other fails to *entirely* link up to any comparably important exhaustive epistemological significance, leaving the other, just this once, inexhaustibly Other. What this means, more concretely, is that the Other cannot be epistemologically pinned down with a degree of exhaustive certainty; the Other is always *partially* occulted and elusive. Given the noumenal existence of this epistemologically irrecoverable residuum at the core of the Other, this Levinasian Other could be said to be constitutionally recalcitrant to a full epistemological uptake on our part. The Other, Levinas tells us, cannot be comprehended, encompassed, assimilated, or absorbed. Hence the persistence of that all but irrepressible question (I do think that this question can usefully be brought up yet again): is there *really* an experience of the Other?

– Levinas goes out of his way (in *Totality and Infinity* especially) to insist upon what, in the final analysis, we might agree to call a somewhat elusive conception of the self. This self overspills all the plastic forms – the literal faces or expressions – we present of it. This self of the Levinasian Other, does not add up to his expression. Expression is not the total removal of the veil. The occult marrow of the noumenon lurks behind the phenomenon. What, then, is the real value of the notion of expression that Levinas finds it necessary to constantly invoke? It at least puts us in touch with the location of an epistemologically uncaptured, ethically accusatory Other. (A similar epistemological sanity regarding the limits of intersubjective cognition is often to be found in medieval mysticism, where, of course, it is God rather than the finite other who, it is urged, has to be loved rather than – *per impossible* – known.)

– *The Limits of Knowledge and the Phenomenology of Dead Objects*: It is – certainly for Levinas – an evident phenomenological fact that one cannot wholly know the other *as* other. Levinas is perhaps at his most straightforward on this point in *Time and the Other*, where he can be found admitting that: 'If one could possess, grasp and know the other, it would not be other'[7]. Such is, perhaps, the most obvious facet of the outer life as it is explored by Levinas. One does not, Levinas insists, wholly experience the *other* in the phenomenological analysis of the play of lights. Nevertheless, Levinas also wants to maintain that the world is obviously *not just* an unpopulated and anonymous miasma of representations, impressions, *vorstellung*, synthesized manifolds, intentional objects or bundled together sense data (call them what you will: philosophers have). *Expression*, therefore, indicates but it does not entirely reveal the Other; so much for the possibility of *total* knowledge of all fragments comprising the orbiting mosaic of reality. Yet notwithstanding the supposedly evident limitations of expression, it shouldn't be dismissed: it still gives us something crucial.

– There is no immediate authentication of the other's credentials to stretch over the epistemological interval between presentation and acknowledgement. (Except, perhaps, love, in the sense that Simone Weil understands it.) Credentials, as their name suggests, have to be believed in.

– If the Cartesian *Cogito – Cogito Ergo Sum* – is dubitable, after all, then Descartes' "evil demon" in the *Meditationes de prima philosophia*, like Socrates' peculiar daemon in the *Apology*, can forever say no, without ever saying: *yes*.

– In the desolate absence of God, a largely assumed doctrine upon which Nietzsche's *On the Genealogy of Morals* incontestably pivots, it can *only* be human beings who are left to judge. (Making a pleonasm of the term 'human values'.) The standards that human beings hold to judge each other can be seen to be lower or higher in nature ("noble" or "base" in Nietzsche's discriminatory vocabulary). It seems reasonable to say that Nietzsche simply throws in his lot with the nobles at the very beginning. *To deny the partisan, to deny this inequality, is to implicitly suppose that God still exists.*

– Nietzsche's ingenuity lay partly in his understanding that to escape the cultural dispirititness of contemporary nihilism, European man still needs a motivating cultural and a personal goal. (Far from stigmatizing the Christian church as nihilistic, Nietzsche candidly admits that virtue and the Church once provided supreme meaning and beauty. He still regards the Catholic Church as providing mankind with some of its most beautiful figures.) The principal goal that Nietzsche somewhat imprudently settled on gives us, however, only a rather ill-polished and *ad hoc* figure: the *Übermensch*. We need not dwell here on finding a specific – let alone a correct – meaning of Nietzsche's inchoate notion of the *Übermensch*: at once a way of cancelling and of mastering humanity within humanity itself. Irrespective, then, of whether or not Nietzsche provides us with any servicable definition of the *Übermensch* in his texts (I do not believe he does), it appears perfectly true that the idea of the *Übermensch* also functions as a kind of *selective affirmation* of the human and one that is, as such, incompatible with the very different Nietzschean thrust towards a univeral affirmation of the entire cosmos as we find it in, above all, his notion of *Amor Fati*. This *Amor Fati*, a neo-Spinozistic embrace of Freud's 'reality principle', is tacitly contained in many other of Nietzsche's ideas too, such as *the Innocence of Becoming*, the idea of the *Dionysian* and that of *Eternal Recurrenence of the Same*. One symptom of precisely this internal Nietzschean clash between Nietzsche's *selective affirmation* and Nietzsche's commitment to the *affirmation of reality* is that, despite the prominence of *Amor Fati*, highly discriminatory typologies, classifications and hierarchies (such as that between man and overman and that between noble and slave) clearly remain essential to Nietzsche. The problem of 'universal affirmation' irreconcilably clashes with the valorization of one select entity in the universe (the *Übermensch*). There is, in addition, a *further* problem *internal* to *universal affirmation* itself, or at least internal to the way *universal affirmation* is conceived of by Nietzsche. (Nietzsche's affirmation, on one view, might legitimately be seen not so much as Spinozistic but as a more historically local problem of reversing Schopenhauer's 'renunciation' of everything in existence. Nietzsche imbibed the principle of the ubiquity of pain from Schopenhauer but subverted its pessimistic tendencies by – unwisely? – claiming that pain can always be mastered and overcome.) For as soon as we move in the general direction of exploring what the advocacy of universal affirmation – *Amor Fati* – might mean in more detail, then the universality of Nietzschean affirmation appears *internally undermined* by an aspect of Nietzsche's human elitism. *Universal affirmation implicitly retro-selects only he who is, in fact, capable of such affirmation.*

– Nietzsche recurrently claims that pain and endurance and even the supposed *mastery* of pain – the terms "harnessing" or "overcoming" are frequently deployed by Nietzsche – is key to (his fantasy of) a painless and meaningful future. But we are, nonetheless, in reality, embodied; we are creatures of tissue – a tissue that is, and must remain, a flag of pain. (If we weren't such creatures, Plato's reference to man as a featherless *biped* and Aristotle's definition of man as a rational *animal* would have made little sense.) Nietzsche did think pain could always be overcome – but this is an obviously absurdly optimistic presupposition, which seems to me not only openly implausible but also wholly indemonstrable. Could it not, as an alternative to this a kind of vastly over-optimistic oversimplification, be the case that there are physical, psychological, or biological limits to what can, in reality, be affirmed by human beings, either as a species or as individuals? Aren't there degrees of physical or even psychological pain that are incapacitating – that lead to, or rather *cannot lead out of*, a total absorption in that pain? I believe this to be so and a variety of subsequent philosophers have agreed, holding the view that there are certain limits to what can be borne by embodied human beings. And you surely cannot affirm what you cannot endure. Or you cannot affirm if incapacitating physical or mental pain absorbs, agitates or sufficiently disturbs, you. I take this to be one aspect of Adorno's proclamation that there is no poetry after Auschwitz and one important sense of Freud's recognition that the reality principle is of necessity sometimes breached in psychosis. If, as Nietzsche contends, the genealogical study of man aims to be nothing more than a piece of clear-sighted animal psychology (*Tierpsychologie*), then we must ask *why* and *upon what grounds* wouldn't it accept as an initial principle that not only the physical but also the mental powers of man can be corrupted by extreme suffering – the kind of severe suffering that can eventually, and sadly, infantilise us. Our conclusion must be that the Nietzschean reinterpretation of suffering, therefore, simply presupposes a prior interpreting subject that is *a-priori* effectively immune to the corrosive effects of unbearable pain.

– The flesh of the body is the limit of its pain.

– Infinitely precious, we live, owing to circumstances, in the decay of fortitude; being almost nameless in our solitude.

– *For the chapter coolly entitled, "Moral Life of the Newspaper Reader"*: According to certain of our cherished institutions – Nietzsche attentively called the press a 'permanent false alarm' – 'ethical living' has now idiosyncratically come to mean (even to otherwise perceptive people), not how you treat people more or less close to you; nor even just how much carbon you might release into the atmosphere; but rather *your attitude* to how much carbon you release. You may or may not already have a small tribe of children, petroleum guzzling cars and ecologically incredibly consequential dogs but, regardless of any or all – or the absence of any or all – of these real consequences, ask for a bag to carry your groceries home with in certain shops and you will be rewarded with a threatening glare. The request itself is, obviously, far from a real index of your carbon emissions. In any case, the whole phenomenon and its vocabulary involves an unwholesome neo-puritan debasement of the concept and the history of *ethics* as it has been developed within philosophical and religious institutions and a self-deluding, self-serving and self-publicizing ideological apparatus for: 1) Reinforcing the good feelings the middle-class ego has about itself and the, on one level, enviable trophies of its publicly accessible lifestyle. 2) Transferring entirely expected human feelings and equally natural human ascetic taboos away from a religious context (you would practically be denounced from today's version of the pulpit for living religiously) and into a supposedly secular but actually eco-onto-theological one.

– When justice itself becomes incomprehensible, the authority, shadowy and obscure, we leave the realm of Kant (where the ultimate authority is, of course, supposed to be oneself) and enter that of Kafka. There is no solitude in Kafka, hence the vague feeling that an abortive and fateful transmissibility of what appears to be a very wide human tradition is taking place, or rather, somehow failing to properly take place, not entirely unlike the impenetrable edifice of the Jarndyce vs. Jarndyce case in Dickens' *Bleak House*, where the single sprawling case can be a moral emblem of Invisible Law and where the ultimate authority is, of course, not oneself but always outside oneself; the self is, or is insofar as it trusts in Law, entirely dependent on the perplexities of the exterior: 'outside influence'. I think it was Schiller, who, under a Kantian influence in *On the Aesthetic Education of Man*, said that the experience of law is the beginning of personality. In Dickens, however, the acceptance and subordination of the individual to the experience of Law is the beginning of the personality's utter breakdown.

– Louis Ferdinand Céline's tortured excitability, in *Journey to the End of Night*, obsessed as he is by female beauty, couldn't be starker. Céline instinctively feels himself entitled to strikingly beautiful women and his very occasional successes in this area then reinforce the sense of entitlement that more often than not then isolates him with a pervading sense of abandonment. He is not immune to beauty. Far from it. He is soon enslaved and writing is his sole mode of "autonomy".

– *The World as Will and Representation* passes successively from the topic of perceptual representation on to metaphysics, then on to ethics, to aesthetics and from aesthetics the text finally settles on proposing a conclusive state of asceticism (also called "denial of the will"). The final Schopenhauerian subject of history therefore becomes *désengagé*. This closing transition to the invocation of the great ascetic silence – Schopenhauer's deep theory – had been (understandably) held in reserve by Schopenhauer from the beginning and it only explicitly emerges in the final book of *The World as Will and Representation*, where what seems to be suggested might be seen as an eventual teleological abandonment of the ethical itself. 'Renunciation', as it is conceived of in the final book of *The World as Will*, seemingly advocates the complete closure of your relationship to the world, an abandonment of the will. As a consequence, you would lose interest in the world as it appears, including, *eo ipso*, the world of the Other. (For interest depends upon an involvement of the will.) Asceticism, therefore, runs the moral risk of blinding you to the problems, sufferings and needs of Others. The ultimate theoretical consequence of following this line of thinking abandonment to its conclusion is that ethics, although, no doubt, still of considerable importance to Schopenhauer, can no longer be said to be of *fundamental importance* within the framework of Schopenhauer's philosophy. Ethics cannot be of overriding importance any longer since it is only related to man's final goal as a *means* and is not internally related to the goal in itself. (That asceticism and ethics are perhaps not the same thing is hinted at in Hume's slighting reference to the 'monkish virtues' and in Adam Smith's brusque reference to them as 'pseudovirtues'.) The ultimate *practical* consequence of following this line of thinking would be to rein in full asceticism of the most extreme Schopenhauerian type on moral grounds and, perhaps, instead hover in *Gelassenheit*.

– What one may call, according to a strictly Levinasian vocabulary, the interrupting force of ethics, *interrupts even philosophy itself*! A predictable objection here would be that this is one interruption too far. Existence; politics – yes, these can interrupt (this could result in an 'engaged philosophy'); the scientific project – yes, absolutely (this could lead the way to a naturalised epistemology or naturalised phenomenology); but a philosophy under the sway of ethics – no! I wonder whether this bridling on our part signals an insecurity in our moral sense of who we are, an insecurity only managing to be partially suppressed by our overconfidence.

– At the utter mercy of the Other, we may not only be inconvenienced and find ourselves impinged upon but also find ourselves prone to unpredictable and even Sadistic threats. And it may even be that Ordinary Language itself can be unpredictable, hideously deceptive (to some) and even threatening (to others). (It was Harold Pinter's plays that amply demonstrated this, as if it needed demonstration.) But are these facts alone enough for us to give up on the constant moral warfare that we wage upon a certain turn of scepticism?

– It is an entirely natural state of the other to be epistemologically reticent: to find himself unable not to shelter his concealed residuum. (This is an altogether too brief attempt to clarify Levinas' complex idea of the 'Transcendence of the Other'.) One shouldn't hold this essentially inaccessible nature against the Other or against philosophy in general. (If generality here isn't precisely the problem.) I'm reminded, in a literary register, of Harold Pinter's match-seller and of Herman Melville's Bartleby, the unaccountable sovereign.

– Restricting the very scope of knowledge's competence – in modernity, usually interpreted as a Kantian gesture – isn't the admission of failure so much as it represents a realistic attempt at a formulation of the structure of the real. (This is also an effort to clarify Wittgenstein's idea of "constitutional limits" to knowing the Other.)

– Transcendence, memory, thought: a closed realm: but *affliction...*? Sympathy is, in a sense, "incomplete": it reaches out, toward suffering, it is not afraid of – it presupposes some form of – 'substitution' (Kant used this term in relation to our knowledge of the Other in the *Critique of Pure Reason*).

– If philosophy in general is purportedly unable to approach the suffering of others, as has occasionally been claimed, one naturally has to ask: how *can* one appreciate the suffering of others? Answer: not philosophically.

– Only *sympathy* – or something very much like it – allows the traversal of the scission of scepticism.

– Subjective suffering, metaphysical separation and our "natural" falling apart into two Cartesian units (body and mind), might be said to all conspire together to present us with the illusion of a philosophical problem: *we cannot know the suffering of the Other.* Our ontological allocation limits us epistemologically. Yet we are or at least *we should be* ethically impressed in any encounter with another – the other appears as solicitation, as hunger and appeal; as widow, orphan and stranger – even as we are existentially waylaid. We should be ethically impressed to the extent that epistemic doubts raised and recurring in philosophy specifically with regard to others are themselves morally as well as theoretically objectionable misconstruals of a *metaphysical situation* of finitude as an *epistemological problem* of limitation.

– God has truly made us in his own image: unknowable.

– Language: the voice of man in God.

– The human body is itself already the doorway to the transcendental, a stepping-stone to the hidden world.

– A wholly removed and entirely private subjectivity, a "purely" detached subjectivity, like that core of unapproachable 'inwardness' peculiar to certain of the writings of Søren Kierkegaard: this subjectivity is mysteriously unfathomed; unaffected by arbitrary tongue and conventional idiom, essentially unaffected by history and by the social world. But from where, then, does this subjectivity receive his lexis or his voice? The intellect does not have a foreign accent.

– The sensuous human voice – characterized by Hegel as 'the element of immediate existence'[6] – is actually – at least it is when it seeks comprehension – infected by the mediate. That is to say, voice, at least when it enters language, reveals the necessity of the reality of the letter; and the letter cannot be compressed into an iterable unit by a removed and private subjectivity, i.e. a subjectivity without either community or history. Plato already knew this but it is two modern philosophers, Wittgenstein in the *Philosophical Investigations* and Derrida in *Of Grammatology*, who have perhaps shown us this in especially rich conceptual and historical detail. Yet one wonders, at this point, whether it could still be objected that referring to a pre-reflective – hence pre-linguistic – self-consciousness (such as that Sartre believed in) could perhaps even now be part of a way to vitiate such a linguistic based attack upon – or self-styled deconstruction of – the self.

– Nietzsche, Schopenhauer, Wittgenstein and Cavell have all, in their different kinds of philosophical texts, recalled men to their forgotten bodies; a call that men then respond to, with those same forgotten bodies. There is, in any case, no other way to respond.

– Entering into the realm of language (by speaking or by writing, for example) is also entering into a form of judgment. In accordance with this thought, it is to be noted here that Abraham (as depicted by Kierkegaard in *Fear and Trembling*) doesn't struggle to work himself free from or to struggle to rise above ordinary langauge. He simply remains (extraordinarily) silent. It is further worthy of note that Abraham's physical expression as well as his verbal communication *must* also be wholly inscrutable if that silence of his is to remain effective. Abraham's *physical expression*, if he is to avoid the misfortune of becoming a mime, has to be an imperceptible correlate of a clandestine and wholly inviolable inwardness. Not only is Abraham silent, therefore, he is also presumably physically expressionless: blank; mechanical; unreadable; illegible.

– Acceptance has its limits and what one does to one's nervous system in the solitude of sleepless nights is *as nothing* compared to the traumas that "friendly" reality bestows upon it in the daytime, the sun.

– We atone for the flame so as to expiate the sun. Plato's men, under a yellower, expanding sun, scream for the shadows. (Away from the star, we are frozen in sunlight.)

– The rumour of daylight hits the denizens of Plato's cave with an avarice that they cannot control. I feel the sun scorching my face without relief. The blistering heat of the sun bewilders me. Not my sun: theirs.

– 'Height' is, in part, so crucial a concept to the ethical thought of Levinas because it is relatively rare to hear Others invoked by someone who does not instantly regard himself – however philanthropically – as their better. Yet if we are indeed losing sight of the heightened moral value of others, it may be because of our immersion in a too ordinary or too secular existence. Hence the essential importance, for Levinas at least, of submitting yourself to the externality of a vector of ultra-mundane religious ritual. (Although the theological dimension of Levinas' thinking is actually more ambiguous than many of his commentators are liable to admit.) One intricate accomplishment of Levinas' *Totality and Infinity* – for which Kant's moral proof of God can be seen as a preparation – is that of establishing the possibility of reconstructing monotheistic religion as well as ethics on a foundation other than that of ontology. In his mature work, Levinas therefore stipulates with a singular degree of clarity the (fundamentally Kantian, as is readily admitted by Levinas himself) creed that religious ritual is, as such, a daily preparation for a rigorous persistence in the ethical realm of separate subjective entities: ritualism is a method and discipline of the morals with which it is associated and to which it leads. The *earlier* approach taken by Levinas toward religion, however, is significantly different. It is tentatively set out in the short text *De l'évasion* and what is most prominently atypical about the position here in *De l'évasion* is the idea that religious ritualism, as such, is not merely preparatory to the good but that in itself it has an *intrinsically* ethical function. One way to make sense of this (earlier) position in *De l'évasion* is to suppose that, like Kantian religious hope, Levinasian ritualism is morally necessary precisely to the same extent as morality itself (and precisely because of the necessity of morality itself).

– Needless to say (is it? *must* I say it? What should I say?), in addition to the optimally expressive metonymous dimension of the human body – the face – of he whom Levinas would call "the other" prompting our proper – or improperly unconditional, or excessive or infinite – ethical comportment, do not Christians *also* look, over a distance of two thousand years, to the face of Christ?

– Nietzsche was nothing if not unfair. But he was being particularly unsporting in calling Kant's Deity 'a hangman's God' in *Twilight of the Idols*. The shadow of the hangman is, in reality, smuggled in by Nietzsche. I cannot recall a single mention of the *summum malum* in Kant – *Nietzsche witches all this into Kant's mouth.*

– One sometimes thinks of the recurring anxiety about the role and the efficacy of the sceptic's voice that is strewn throughout the writing of Levinas (already in the first sentence of *Totality and Infinity*). And the same anxiety finds voice throughout the later writings of Wittgenstein – this is not least so in the reactions – and there is little that could be more important to the flow of language than the reactions of one's fellow language users – of the abnormal pupil in the *Philosophical Investigations*: a deviant adder, a glib bully, a profound child: a downright spoilsport.

– We owe *so* much to science. Some of us owe our lives. (Obviously, I'm thinking of the substantial advances of medical science, in particular, here.) How are we to live these lives? We shouldn't peevishly hold it against science (as Kierkegaard did, especially in his *Journals*) that it does not answer all of the questions in our lives; it has already, very often, saved them.

– A picture is worth a thousand words, many of them lies. Basic aesthetico-moral assumption: deception.

– The Truth does not insist on being told. (This is an entirely different, though related, point to: the facts don't speak for themselves.) *Those who have abandoned Truth must watch their words.* (In an entirely different way to those who seek to express the acceptable face of truth. For it does have an unacceptable face, too.)

– Philosophy, which does at least speak for itself, appears also to love itself. But let's not bother to deny that love is, amongst other things, also, agony and incessant interrogation. If you love someone enough, you want to give him or her some sort of ultimatum, don't you?

– The unity of a face is *integrated* in its expression.

– Expression: the obliteration of form. No one has told us this better than Schopenhauer and Levinas. (To be fair, no one has tried.)

– The essence of expression is emotion. Otherness is caught in expression and beyond each expression there hovers the limit of another transcendence.

– *"Where are you going now?" Harry asks. "To put a cardigan on",
Phillipa says. "A cardigan?" "Yes." "A bloody cardigan?" "Yes, a
bloody cardigan!" "Why?" "Because I'm cold, of course." "We all are."*

– Wittgenstein straightforwardly declares that: 'An animal
cannot point to the thing that interests it'[8] and I've seen this kind
of claim routinely repeated by others. But it does not seem to be
obviously true. (Wittgenstein's claim isn't one that applies to *all*
non-human animals.) I can perfectly remember the time an affec-
tionate Labrador once pointed – *I can think of no better word for it*
– out a foxhole to me, twice. Aren't some dogs even *called*
pointers?

– It may even be worth asking here whether one could imagine
specific cases in which a dog's non-response to your particular
words itself informed you that you were using the right or the
wrong words e.g. him or her not answering to what you thought
was his or her name. For a dog's reaction or rather – as in this
case – his non-reaction can function as a criterion of correctness
where language use is concerned. Perhaps one also thinks here of
some basic *inter-species performatives*. This term (made up on the
spot) is meant to refer to verbal performatives used in the
process of basic dog-training, for example. (Wittgenstein has
already provided perfectly adequate answers to those who
would question whether a language of orders was a complete
language.) Incidentally, this idea of a dog's non-response or
response correcting you on linguistic use stands directly
opposed to the somewhat doctrinaire position of L. Feuerbach,
who repeatedly stressed that epistemological correction *must
derive from members of our own species.*

– What if Wittgenstein used the example of dog trainers instead
of shoppers and builders in the opening of his *Philosophical
Investigations*?

– The boundary between nature and the human is oftentimes guarded by man's best friend, the dog. There can be little honest doubt that the human bond with nature is most proximately mediated in its intersubjective form in our interaction with dogs, who are essentially wolves with their instantaneous anti-human antagonism bred out. Not many animals apart from *canis lupus familiaris* look you in the eye. No other animal looks so intently at the left, or the *most expressive*, part of your face. *Nota Bene.* On the whole, Schopenhauer's persuasive remarks upon the reality of canine expression – e.g. it primarily occurs *in the tail* – make a lot more sense than do Wittgenstein's.

– *"If myrmecology has taught me anything,"* Harry states, *"it is this: animals are republicans by nature – though ants and bees are monarchists." "I have my doubts, Harry." "Yes, because you are ill-informed."*

– *"Harry, you're intolerable." "You are clearly exaggerating, again. Another demonstrable untruth has managed to escape from your beautiful lips." "Do you hate me, Harry?" "Not yet." Instead of laughing, or even shouting, she makes as though to slap him but is internally distracted and lets her hand twist about his personal space like a gymnast's ribbon in a slow, neurotic descent. "Harry, Don't you think before you speak?" " Oh no, I try to find quieter times for my reflection".*

– The majority of some of the most intuitively appealing modern philosophical accounts of "encountering the other" are underpinned by an acceptance that our 'sense' or our 'sentiment' – not our *knowledge* but rather our *non-conceptual experience* (more idiomatically, our *feeling*) of, say, sympathy (Schopenhauer), respect (Kant), responsibility (Levinas), love (Feuerbach), acceptance (Gabriel Marcel) or acknowledgement (Cavell) – of otherness is overwhelming, overpowering; leaves us pained, somehow inescapably in debt to them. Levinas goes to the extreme of claiming that we are actually *hostage* to the other – which more than merely hints at some serious hazard in our position. Nietzsche, too, of course, likes, more often than not, to invoke – and sometimes likes to avoid – the idea that ceding something to his philosophical writing is very dangerous – which hints, sometimes a touch preposterously, at certain, largely unspecified, sublime heights. (But when *I* think of danger, I think of a loose roof tile.) (Is this reassuring? To whom?)

– If we are held *hostage* to the other's demand, invitation, solicitation, accusation or appeal, then all communication with the Other is risky from the outset, for it suggests – Levinas is explicit in admitting this – not only that the exigency is infinite in length but that our inwardness is unseated or broken with the force of trauma. This reflects the impact of an Other, the effect of the attempted uptake of the aura of expression. The Other even makes us who we are: Levinas obliquely hints that the ethical agent is himself constituted in the process of being subjected to ethical exigencies. And if we truly cannot do enough to ameliorate the conditions of the other ('An awakening that never stops') then, alongside the most unblinking devotees of Jeremy Bentham, we might hand over ultimate responsibility to a faceless arithmetic that admits that there is no obvious *limit* to *maximizing* the happiness of others.

– *"What would I do without you Harry?" "Oh, I expect you'd find a substitute." "There is no substitute." "Of course there is. That's what the bloody word means."*

– From the outside, you've always looked like an insider.

– *"Let me tell you something Harry." "I've already been told*

something earlier, thanks all the same Phillippa." "And I used to think
you had no sense of humour." "A characteristic lack of imagination on
your part." Her stony face expressed a certain reservation: she saw
things differently.

– Schopenhauer had little time for understatement: 'The brain
and its consciousness isolates human individuals'[9], he writes (in
accordance with the position of the later Feuerbach). Yet it might
be pointed out that the separation of individuals and presumably
the latent potential therein for the possibility of scepticism
alluded to here is also the very *source* of our salvation. It is not
that your experience is limited, but rather that Human
Experience itself is intrinsically physically – metaphysically, even
– limited. (These are no doubt the same 'constitutional limits' to
knowledge that Wittgenstein liked to speak of.) Why we should
seek to overcome that metaphysical limitation metaphysically is
not necessarily itself a metaphysical question. Our epistemological limits invite us to transcend them ethically, as in the case
of our epistemological limits, which impede knowledge of, but
not faith in, the existence of God.

– The production of infinity actually *requires* our initial
separation.

– *Phillipa, practically at one with the black dress that she wore, opened*
and – "goodbye!" – closed the door. Alone, she was lovable.

– The body is the shape of the desire to be happy.

– There is nothing clearly and particularly stipulative about the
moral authority of the other (except perhaps in limited cases: an
injured man lies dying of thirst). There they are (they are, in fact,
just the first ones to be there), they have come along, they have
inconvenienced us; we are incommoded and their presence

detains us. We are waylaid. Yet although some sort of response is demanded of us and is, indeed, unavoidable (since avoiding or ignoring the Other *is itself a response*) it is generally not entirely clear what *specific* response is demanded of us. Nor (and this is always true) is there anything, in particular, that our response to the situation of the other can be totally covered by. That is to say, there isn't any one thing that our "duty" would be completely discharged by. As this complex point may also be put: one can always do more to help.

– I'm at the top of the staircase on the top floor landing. Everything is closed. I try the doors a second time: all locked. A telephone rings one floor below me. I run downstairs in a panic. There's no answer. I hammer the door again. The phone inside the apartment keeps ringing. I make a ridiculous figure of myself by frantically trying the handle: as it's open anyway, I'm thrown into the room. In a chair by the window, directly facing me, is someone smoking a cigarette. She just lets this interruption occur: interesting woman.

– *Dasein* was dosed to the very spangle-point of pain's obliteration, the removal of the chief impediment to a form of happiness radiating outwards from within. Within: without.

– *Dasein* speaks: "Opiates commemorate – with a dull, comforting, bruise – the obliteration of memory, recollection's blank withdrawal."

– *Harry hears the front door slamming behind her. "Is it you?" "Yes, it's me." "Where have you been?" "Out with Kate again." "Kate. She really is very unengaging Phillipa. She's always reading books with titles like: The Fragility of Dissent." "So what?" "Fragility, I'll grant you. I've no problem with Fragility. Fragility would be a theme accepted without the slightest demur by any panel in the land. But*

Dissent?" "You could say the exact opposite as well." "I could." "But you don't." "Precisely." "I don't see what precision has got to do with it." "You don't see what precision has got to do with anything, Phillipa." "No, quite right Harry: approximation is my rule of thumb. As suitable a rule as any for an ailing mankind."

– And, in the denial of night, the repudiation of circumstance: imagination, enemy of despair.

– "Constitutional Limits Revisited": With regard to others, we do not know what we never even thought we knew.

– Why does it ever occur to anybody to seriously make this claim of solipsism with any conviction? Short answer: it doesn't.

– Schopenhauer discovered, with a certain empiricist sanity, that we are called out of the incredibly fanciful hypothetical fiction of a philosophical solipsism by an entirely naturally occurring *sympathy for the other* (sympathy of a kind perhaps previously best captured by the moral sentimentalist Francis Hutcheson). Sympathy is a natural moral horizon, as it were: a given of *our* condition as humans. (Or a given of our *condition* as normal humans. Or a given of our ordinary condition as *normal* humans.) Irrespective, therefore, of some of its more outlandish metaphysical propositions and some of its epistemological pratfalls, Schopenhauer's systematic philosophy – genuinely approximating the later thought of Levinas in this respect – at least moves us into the general position of needing to offer a Samaritan's help, a help without limit for these others, even though it is also true – for a certain Schopenhauer – that we cannot even competently prove, from a strictly philosophical standpoint, that these others exist (see §19 of the first volume of his *The World as Will and Representation*). Hence it would seem that: after all, the thesis that the Other subject of experience is *primae facie* beyond full epistemological recuperation and recalcitrant to a *philosophical* uptake of any sort also still holds even for Schopenhauer *in some of his moods* (for the concept of exhaustive human expression that Schopenhauer also invokes entirely contradicts this Levinasian position). Yet an inability to disprove the sceptic with a solid theoretical argument does not matter as much as you might think for Schopenhauer (I earlier raised the good fortune of his "empiricist sanity"), insofar as *the overriding passion of sympathy* directed toward the other irresistibly arises within us and, crucially, irresistibly *motivates* us to act. It is *passion* rather than *reason* that is motivationally causal (a view standing in continuity with the basic approach to motivation famously found in Hume). Sympathy, *qua* passion rather than piece of reason, always overrides the mere thought *reasonable* thought of scepticism. Compassion even shows *us* who *we* are: we are not monstrous. Our personal ethical capacities are themselves discovered in our interactions with our neighbour. *Love your neighbour* – this love is (at least a part of) you yourself.

– Under a close and patient analysis, one is ultimately forced to admit that the moral response to scepticism loosely sketched by Schopenhauer in *The World as Will and Representation* – but found better developed in Levinas, Stanley Cavell, Wittgenstein and, no doubt, others – locks Schopenhauer himself into an inescapable logical circle. For the supposed "self-evidence" of Schopenhauer's morality of compassion (i.e. the *passion of sympathy* that overrides any theoretical scepticsm about the Other) and the 'Impartial Other' that is necessarily presupposed, if only tacitly, in any plausible appeal to self-evidence in ethics reciprocally and circularly place and support one another. (As this point may be also be put: Schopenhauer is warranted in claiming the self-evidence that he does for the goodness of sympathy only on the basis of a tacit appeal to the guarantee of impartial scrutineers: others.) (One might be a little venturesome here and say that the 'Impartial Spectator' of Adam Smith represents and ideally expresses the later development of the Feuerbachian species.) Intersubjectivity and Morality are thereby interlocked within the horizon of the Schopenhauerian system. Morality creates – in this circular fashion – the conditions for assuming and actually acting for – one remembers Wittgenstein saying that *pity* is a *form of conviction* – an Other subjectivity. This is surely an example of the *interdependency* of each of the elements of his philosophy that Schopenhauer was conceptualising in describing his own work as an organic whole and not as a foundational system such as that of Descartes. The beginning of *The World as Will and Representation* therefore already presupposes the end; and the end already presupposes the beginning.

– Although it might be initially tempting to avoid the historical issues and stubbornly remain in the *nunc stans*, it may, overall, be worth further inviting some fresh air and noting that the kind of deliberate rupture or opening up of one's own isolated monad of moral subjectivity to such "impartial scrutineers" as Schopenhauer implicitly suggests is also famously figured in Hegel's acknowledgement that we should relinquish an exclusively assertive individual right to determine the good and instead embrace the general public understanding of the ethical (*Sittlichkeit*), an ethical life that is located in concrete human institutions and, as such, transcends caprice and whimsy outright. In Summa: in order to be able to fundamentally secure the self-evident goodness of sympathy (that Schopenhauer relies upon so as to connect with, in acting for, the Other) it will be necessary to refer to at least the *possibility* of correction and hence also the prespposed *existence* of Others. The movement of ethical institution is not linear but circular. Ethics cannot be stepped into from the *outside*.

– Figures such as the Impartial Spectator make mistakes in moral decision-making in principle *rectifiable*.

– Ethics can straightaway be characterised as *responsiveness*, which straightaway commits one to opposing the extreme version of the Fichtean thesis of subjective idealism. Ethics comes from a *heteronomy* that is, more precisely, the passion of sympathy (I refer here the historically interested reader to the theories of Schopenhauer, the phenomenology of Max Scheler and the empiricism of much of the Scottish Enlightenment – I think especially of Francis Hutcheson and Adam Smith.) For Levinas, working specifically against the dominance of the Heideggerean dispensation (although he is still partly within its phenomenological framework – one only has to think of his persistent interest in the Husserlian structure of intentionality), the History of the Meaning of Being is fissured asunder by a single hungry child. That this child is, indeed, hungry we grasp from immediately seeing – or reading – the expression of her face. A more advanced formula: we know her hunger from her expression – for "face" is, in fact, a metonym for the whole of human bodily expression. We feel something for the human subject that allows no sceptical threats and that always brings us back to the world of empathy and, in principle, an ethical correction by others. (Levinas, in his thought, prefers the term *responsibility* to *sympathy*.) What we are presented with here is an undelegatable relationship to the other that is not preceded by guaranteed existence of the Other but which assumes it, because it is already necessarily accompanied by or hinges upon the existence of others as guarantors of true feeling. Our confidence in our own ethical judgments is always profoundly tied to Other human beings: i.e. the co-presence of self-evidence governed by others themselves. Insofar as one is tempted to tentatively reproach Levinas, one could do so here, in at least insofar as his stress on the *absolute Otherness of the Other* does not appear to easily permit him to grant that Other a role in the formation of the co-presence required for guaranteeing the *self-evidence* of the good. If my relationship to the Other is straightaway one of *difference* and, therefore, one of *deference* —as Levinas does claim: in references to the 'Height' of the Other, for example – then the Other himself, who is already *deferred to*, cannot be impartial. Presumably, Levinas would say in response to this charge that he is interested in the uniqueness of our responsibility and not epistemological guarantees of it. As this point may also be put, this kind of critique of Levinas does not, in itself, jeopardize the consistency of Levinas' insistent concretisation of the ethical situation and his insistence that *some* act has to be undertaken. It only robs the specific act undertaken of epistemological guarantees of a self-evidently good character. Or Levinas might take a far more radical and more philosophically hazardous approach and stress that the responsibility in which he is interested has to be teased apart from – because it is entirely different in nature from – such notable phenomena as sympathy, empathy, pity, compassion...

– Morality and Intersubjectivity appear together as two reciprocally supporting elements. This becomes patently obvious in a close reading not only of Schopenhauer but also of the philosophic work of Feuerbach. And although it was indeed Feuerbach who first introduced the following terms (in their contemporary usage) into philosophical writing, it was Martin Buber who memorably took them up and fused them into a succinct and catchy formula: *I and Thou*. – I am not here merely *concocting* a link of questionable provenance between Feuerbach and Levinas!

– Major thinkers of the Scottish Enlightenment, as well as Ludwig Feuerbach, couldn't be more *explicit* in trying to calibrate the findings of the individual conscience with the community view (Feuerbach's residual post-Hegelianism is perhaps most evident here). Levinas, however, appears to maintain that our ethical sense of responsibility arises from a singular experience – the epiphany – of the face or the expression of the Other. But this curious grounding in a primordial and singular experience has – or so Levinas appears to suggest – to be *embedded* within the specific Judeo-Christian tradition, a brave move which arguably brings Levinas back to the recalibration position of Smith and Feuerbach by means of highlighting the traditionally religious aspects of morality (which represents, of course, a reversal of Feuerbach's own method).

– The kingdom of heaven isn't to be submitted to any measurement, however imprecise, by history (or 'epochal' history in the Heideggerean sense). But in the face of this type of Levinasian take on the historical-eschatological directive, ontology – backed, point-by-point, by the pleading triumphalism of human common sense – *seems* to affirm its own privileged urgency. Yet the quintessentially Levinasian idea of a Monotheistic religion 'beyond being' has actually been thoroughly ventilated by a variety of thinkers in recent times generally from the perspective of orthodox (Christian or Jewish) or Catholic paradigms: Jean-Luc Marion, Christos Yannaris, late Derrida, Gabriel Marcel and Gianni Vattimo, for example, irrespective of their significant philosophical differences, might all agree to say with one voice: *God is not a thing.*

– Intersubjectivity and the self-evidence of Morality are inextricably linked by means of the reciprocal support, correction and foundation that they offer one another. Intersubjectivity in particular, has, further, served as the apparent cornerstone of this architectonic of linkage and has notably done so, in terms, for example, of the naturalistic philosophy of Feuerbach (insofar as, in Feuerbach, intersubjectivity has been *already grounded* by means of the introduction of the presupposition of the species).

Feelings of the good need not slide into the suspicion of capricious subjective arbitrariness at all but rather can be recalibrated, when necessary, by Adam Smith's 'Impartial Spectator'; by Feuerbach's species; or by Wittgenstein's community of men training each other.

– The Species has an *epistemologically* more authoritarian nature than the Ego.

– The expressive face is mobile, fluid, changeable. Yet, at least for Levinas (Schopenhauer and Cavell would vociferously disagree at this point), there is an always a point at which the Other becomes *inaccessible*. On the other hand, relinquishing all the Cartesian metaphysical manoeuvres that aimed to enshrine an unrelieved ignorance at the undiscoverable reality of the subject, the philosophers of expression (other than Levinas) with whom we are largely concerned here – Schopenhauer, Wittgenstein and Cavell, for example – enriched the picture of the human soul as a place of constant and helpless bodily expression. Levinas, it is true, travels a great distance with each of them but at a certain spot he stops and steps forwards alone.

– Our natural acknowledging of the facial (and, of course, the bodily) expression of the Other removes epistemological worries that sceptics typically raise about the presence of others. Descartes himself, however, even in the 'hats and cloaks' episode of the *Meditationes de prima philosophia* did not highlight 'the Other' as a specific *kind* of sceptical problem. Nonetheless, it remains significant that Descartes does not record either a human face or the expression of a human body in his sceptical meditations at all. But an expression cannot exist without a face – an absurdity curiously foreseen and developed in Lewis Carroll's Cheshire cat.

– One should not be slighting towards men when picking up on their interest in women's fashion: such an interest, when authentic, isn't automatically to be taken as a symptom of fetishism (neither Freudian sexual fetishism nor Marx's commodity fetishism). In accordance with this polite directive, and in spite of Plato (and Hegel), Nietzsche – in *Schopenhauer as Educator* – actually recommends that the exemplary status of a philosopher should extend to what he *wears* as well as what he *teaches*. (After all, even philosophy has its internal fashions.) To be dapper, to deliberately dress as a dandy, to value style (and, perhaps, appreciate women's fashion) with even a minimally appreciable level of taste does indeed occur among writers situated within the horizon of the philosophical. (Miklos Szentkuthy probably represents this tendency best.)

– Division and discontinuity are responsible for jeopardizing the adequacy of interrelation, for Nature connects as much as she divides.

– Expression is the condition of our ethical interrelation with one another.

– Descartes' initial acceptance of a primarily purely episte-mologcal model of engagment with the Other, of necessity, resisted the stream of thought found in Wittgenstein, Heidegger, Cavell, Schopenhauer and Levinas, which immediately privilges the *non-cognitive* and (in some cases), more narrowly, the *ethical* aspects of our engagement with Others. Descartes' refusal of the face, in the search for the cloak and the hat, embodies a parallel restriction. (We look in vain for peers amongst hats and cloaks.) His hint at a beatific vision at the end of *Meditation III*, however, bespeaks a different Descartes. As he wrote to Mersenne (I quote the letter from memory): 'I have never written about the Infinite except to submit to it.'

– Since the dawn of Cartesian modernity, it has become clear that an additional figure has entered the philosophical lexicon: the *Other*. We do not necessarily require him to recognize us (as in Hegel). Nor is it that we hazily feel his gaze on the horizon of our fundamentally sterile intentionality as a secondary, though equally blank, focus of reference (Sartre). Nor is he just required to train us in the practice of following the rules of our language (Wittgenstein). Nor, even, is it that his vigilant questioning draws up answers from within us that we simply could not have dredged up on our own (Freud); (see also: Plato). What one sees in the enigmatic construal of the reception of the other, particularly intensified in the recent work of Levinas, can also be related to something admittedly less emphatic in many other quintessentially modern philosophers: in certain of the voices found in the fragments of the later writings of Wittgenstein suggesting that the pain words in general circulation are more important than our particular private mental experiences, and also to a certain moment in the critical philosophy of Kant; but perhaps most particularly in Schopenhauer's moral argument against 'theoretical egoism' in §19 of *The World as Will and Representation*. What then perhaps sometimes re-emerges in our contemporary reception of Nietzsche's unsqueamish and unflinching critique of morality is a historically recurring moral discomfort with and epistemological inability to shirk (the unavoidability of) a certain kind of scepticism, and, in particular, its trend toward the exclusion or the neglect of the suffering that we do not know. (The suffering that we do not want to know.)

– Love makes people unforgettable.

– Post-Hegelian thinkers of a certain stripe – Karl Marx and Ludwig Feuerbach are superb examples – can be peculiarly devoted to the human species. A curious equivocation concerning that species, however, possibly even a unique one, is at work throughout the writings of Nietzsche. For Nietzsche is at once (at least at times) an arch-humanist dedicated to the advancement, improvement, beauty and violent thriving of humanity and (at other times) Nietzsche is a despondent, detached anti-humanist indifferent to, or even (at the limit), enthralled by and enthusiastic about, its utter obliteration. Nietzsche, with an air of emphasized finality (and an enviable lack of self-doubt), points out that: *'Many species of animal have already disappeared. If man should disappear as well, nothing would be lacking in the world.'*[10] Nietzsche is at once Voltaire and De Sade.

– *Elegy For the End of a Species*: Schopenhauer's *The World as Will and Representation* – where the Kantian noumenon is prepared to be step by step phased into the Unconscious – is dramatic in its overall architecture rather than being, say, either dialectical or expository. And if *The World as Will and Representation* is thus conceived of as a vast four-act play (a view for which there is some lively precedent), then the core protagonist of *The World as Will and Representation* is not to be considered as *Geist*, nor productive labour, nor the history of *Sein*. The core protagonist of Schopenhauer's drama is, rather, something more reminiscent of *Thanatos*: the death-drive: that which precipitates "autosublation" (a term of Schopenhauer-interpretation that I actually have access to only *via* the writings of Peter Szondi), by which term I mean the auto-obliteration of the entire universe, which requires but one single species to bring it about: *homo sapiens*. The gesture of obliteration oddly restores to man the ontological privilege that he had been denied at the very start of the Schopenhauerian drama. (Man had famously utterly lost his status as a unique subject of idealism when Schopenhauer took an entomological approach to finding an "archaic" subjective correlate of objective reality.)

– Zarathustra IV: Exegeses, Commentaries, Remarks – One might, perhaps, begin (one surely has to begin; where can one begin?) by questioning the repeated attempts (notably by P. Loeb and, in a recent essay, Walter Brogan) to show that Nietzsche's *Thus Spoke Zarathustra* cannot be very easily or naturally understood as the deepening narration of a tragedy[11]. Commentators such as those mentioned further point out – quite unobjectionably, at this early point of their argument – that the deeply puzzling part IV of *Thus Spoke Zarathustra* stands out most peculiarly from the rest of the text. (As Fink had already been quick to point out.) Since it cannot credibly be envisioned as a tragic narration, part IV – so their argument more contentiously develops – should, therefore, be read as something resembling a modern attempt at an *ancient satire play*. As this point may also be put: part IV – both Brogan and Loeb explicitly claim– is an essentially *comic* take on the preceding three *tragic* elements of the text. But it would not be especially difficult to counter the evidence that Loeb and Brogan offer, for it undoubtedly does not seem extraneous for us to note here, against their case, that the character of Zarathustra is, in any event, *already satirized* and so does not require further mocking within the progress of the poem itself. That is to say, Zarathustra is not pilloried chronologically or sequentially (i.e. not *just* in the final Part IV) so much as he is parodied *synchronically*. Commentators such as Brogan and Loeb have not, therefore, fully appreciated the fact that the character of *his ape* already satirizes the figure of Zarathustra and not just in the final part. Zarathustra's ape: the buffoon who pursues the figure and distorts the teaching of Zarathustra and from whom he is as inseparable as is Othello from his jealousy, Lear from his folly, Oedipus from his fate, Hamlet from his ghost.

– There is nothing immediately charming in *Thus Spoke Zarathustra*: nothing charming, nothing touching, little of the human. To our way of thinking, the narrative style of this lazy classic seems to consist of repeated returns to the beginning: new starts, linked to loosely related literary set pieces serving to deliver one or another – more or less garbled – philosophical lecture. The figures of *Zarathustra* have little fully rounded emotional reality. When examined individually, they possess only a modicum of philosophical significance, which they express exhaustively. If there is a certain naïveté of style in *Zarathustra*, therefore, it is not a touching form of naïveté, it is an ignorantly optimistic one – for example, in its downright cartoonish elision of the ugly truth that extreme pain is existentially restrictive – *and all this in Nietzsche*, where cynicism is more typically the mask for a wider array of cognitive abilities.

– *To the consternation of Sir Thomas Browne*: In what we might regard as the clowning scene of Shakespeare's *Hamlet*, it is the skull of the jester (the figure of the clown, an incarnation of parody, is here disincarnate in the most bald form possible), after all, that Hamlet holds in his hand and asks where his jests are now, only to persist in being confronted, naturally, by the blank radiance of death. Nevertheless, it is perfectly true that Hamlet himself cannot restrain his own sense of humour, which isn't exactly his own: it is Shakespeare's.

– *Phillipa: "Why don't you write something for the theatre, Harry? In fact, I think it's high time you wrote for the theatre." "Theatre, Moi? Ah, the theatre. High time? The bloody theatre. I can't Phillipa. I just can't. [Pause] The thing is, my father was himself a one man theatre, Phillipa, and I still feel fear and pity in his presence."*

– *Phillipa walked out onto the balcony with brisk menthol precision. Wearing just her heels and her kimono, she lit one of her Japanese cigarettes in the dark and hunkered down on her haunches so as to smoke it with idle circumspection, tapping the surplus ash – residue of vanquished breath – into a green leather pouch. Harry watched her through the balcony window. They say that the less you have, the less you have to lose. But (evidently) the less you have, the less you have.*

– Two dense, intricate philosophical texts written partially under the shadow cast by Martin Buber – *Totality and Infinity* and *Otherwise than Being* – testify to a particular form of the encounter with the Other: an *ethical epiphany*. No very precise response is actively stipulated as a direct consequence of this singular encounter in either book. The inexorable appeal generated by what is somewhat ambivalently called an "experience" of the other promises nothing except the guarantee of further appeals. Schopenhauer had already noted the infinite protraction of demands generated from the subject: 'Given that the finite subject is actually an expression of an infinite willing then demands and requests go on to infinity'[11]. It is entirely possible to imagine that part of us immediately bridles at – shrinks from – the presence of endless demands and uninvited but infinite requests being so innocently incurred. An unavowed part of us doubtless feels it to be a crushing burden to be dodged. Such a fundamentally egoistic reticence may be strategically understandable on a psychological level: our *responsibility to the other* is such as to render us, in principle, *incapable* of satisfying its intrusive, inexhaustible requirements and so, in the face of it, we revert to clinging to our own existence all the more firmly (clinging to our will-to-live, as in Schopenhauer). Pillorying the position of Levinas as the overwhelming provocation of responsibility through the pathos of the Infinite might also best be understood strategically, i.e. on a psychological level. The exigency that lays claim to me leads on to infinite demands but, as *moral* exigency, it at first admits of only one answer: "here I am". The use of my indexical "here..." immediately acknowledges the Other as well as pinpointing my own existence.

– 'Supererogatory' is, in reality, little more than a platitudinous term, a sop to a variety of more or less self-serving little secular interests: responsibility is *infinite*.

– The flat and merciless moral summons; it didn't emerge with Kant, of course, it's archaic. I could, I suppose, easily ignore his or her (more or less faint) summons – in point of fact, I often do – but not without thereby incurring... The weak body generates obligations whose murky sanction is visible only on the level of practice.

– Are gifts to be known rather than received? Why should our relation to other objects, let alone our relationship to the Other, be thought of as being primarily a cognitive one (i.e. one of knowledge) rather than one of trust or love or responsibility? (This thought hints at theological echoes in Kierkegaard, as well as ethical echoes in Levinas, Cavell, Simone Weil and others.) The attachment to cognition over responsibility, for Levinas in particular, is already to be read as a symptom of philosophy's automatic but imprudent deference to epistemological concerns. Levinas has enshrined his proposal that we move on from this misplaced deference to the epistemological in his claim that "Ethics is first philosophy".

– Molloy, Murphy, Vladimir, Estragon: enduring, without the chic resolution of an idler, the present. Deferring, more or less patiently, to infinity. What comes to pass – time – passes in the drama of daily conduct. It is not exactly a mistake, therefore, to interpret Samuel Beckett's *Waiting for Godot* in these terms: as consecrating the fact, or the truth, or the time (or the joke), of waiting.

– *Harry thought it might interest the bearded Man in the purple jacket to learn how it was that he and Phillipa had first met. Harry proceeded to tell him that he had initially thought, all those years ago, that it would be fun to play her at chess. "Fun!" the dishevelled Man chuckled, incredulously.*

– Through my tears: the assuaged sky.

– *The Man who sits aside: When Harry had come back to his seat at the table, the bearded man in purple sat to the left hand side of him gripped the hem of the white table cloth with both hands and asked Harry: 'When you just went, could you pee?" "What do you mean?" "Could you go?" "'Go'?" "Yes. Could you go?" "Yes, I went." The man sat next to him at the restaurant table nodded silently. He then laughed quietly and said: "He went! He went alright!" Harry was smiling now: "Why don't you go then?" "Me? Go! That's baseless optimism for you." "Do you have a medical problem?" Harry enquires, very gently. "No. Not a problem exactly. That's not the word I would use. That's not a word I would allow. Not that word at all. I would avoid that word and use quite a different word, quite a different word altogether." "Or none at all?" "Yes. That's it exactly. Quite a different word – or, as you say, none at all". We must imagine Harry grinning broadly, from ear to ear.*

– A philosophical ethics without any psycho-bite; i.e. an ethics that entirely omits the introduction of any intimidation deservedly incurred by the individual subject – Sartre's toothless ethics of incommensurable choices, for example – has, in the ultimate analysis, to be condemned to be nothing but a marionette of human whimsy. Such caprice – as figured in the basic existential model of the self as an inaccessible trigger of unpredictability – certainly isn't much of a basis for an ethical attitude. This is no doubt why ethical empiricists who locate the origins of ethics in the self are then quick to reach out beyond themselves and beyond their own immobilized conscience for someone – an 'Impartial Spectator' – to act as their big guarantor. (We wonder whether Heidegger in *Being and Time*, considered from the point of view of the necessity for morality of the more impartial perspective, is actually able to incorporate precisely this element – that is, we wonder whether Heidegger is able to factor in referral to the promise of a more interpersonal and cooler understanding of our *moral* decisions – as an essential component of individual authentic choice, given that, reading *Being and Time*, one gets the clear impression that, for individual choice, conformity to "The They" would seem to render *Dasein* "inauthentic".)

– *The unkempt man in the purple jacket took two bread rolls out of a baker's white paper bag and handed one over to Harry. Harry and the man in the purple jacket sat next to one another, eating their rolls in silence. Harry had his long black overcoat on. The man in the purple jacket suddenly looked inside his roll, checking for the presence of something untoward, but then carried on eating it, regardless. The park bench overlooked a steep but uninhabited hill. The man began to speak: "Thanks for inviting me." "Bloody parties. It's Phil who insists on having them." "Phillipa is very pleasant." 'Phillipa... She's Welsh. Her father's name was Gwilym ap Llewelyn. Superb name." "Welsh princess obtained, Welsh princess retained" the man in the purple jacket concluded to his own satisfaction, crumpling up the white paper bag and popping it in his jacket pocket. Suddenly, he leapt to his feet, spat out the bread roll and started violently coughing. He was like this for about three minutes or so: stooped, hawking, gasping and staring accusingly at both Harry and, behind him, the wintry sun.*

– Sympathy for the Other secures an *immediate* warrant for our moral actions toward him. His very expressions spark the sympathy that secures that legitimacy. (Our pity is already a form of the 'conviction' that Wittgenstein spoke of.) Let me restate this in a more epistemological formula: there is no mischievous homunculus inside the belly or the brain doing a fugitive – but all the more real – wince. (Or, take fear as an example. The fantasy element here is that of distilling out from the dry mouth and the increased rate of the pulse, an *essence* of 'fear' that is separate from the horrible restlessness the man feels.)

– Sympathy in itself *seems* incomplete – it reaches out. *But so do people.*

– I thought to myself (to who else?) that desires glimmer not deep within or behind but *in the shine on* the surface of her green eyes, on the tight flesh of her taut white neck. Wittgenstein and Schopenhauer, Levinas and Cavell, all supply evidence for this. Irrespective of a myriad of technical philosophical differences, all four philosophers are in harmony on this detail: at one point in the history of Western philosophy, a single metaphysical factor – specifically, an ill-starred Cartesian ontology of minds and bodies – radically interfered with an effective – *expressivist* – response to scepticism. (Scepticism never goes unchallenged.) As this point may also be put, any philosophy that takes the first anti-sceptical step by looking beyond the face and body for another *mind* has already ontologically situated itself towards the sceptical question in such a way as to make any solution to it impossible *ab initio.*

– *Being judged to be capricious or self-serving:* Such a peril as this threatens every subjective morality and, indeed, every basically morally sentamentalist undertaking that, necessarily rooted in subjectivity, remains rigorously isolationist – that of Shaftsbury in his *Characteristics of Men, Manners, Opinions, Times,* is probably the best example.

– The Other need not always be at all reticent about coming into contact with us and indeed can even seem clamorous and not a little urgent.

– The Other is a breath of fresh air from the great indoors.

– Gazing without light at the bathroom mirror, I was left to the night-time tide. In the mirror (on its surface): I saw the lip of the backward abyss. I see nothing but the eternal and the abrupt, the second lip of the abyss.

– Let us take this occasion to recall certain details of our intricately half-forgotten lives and term these cherished details *the moments we stole back from time.* We already know by now that certain instants, particular times and themes, are effaced without remainder in the grandest of the metaphysical systems of development (the worthless totality of a Hegel, for example). Yet after everything has been seemingly accounted for by the warmly panoramic view of a cosmic Hegel or a more concrete, global Marx, there remain behind the sprawling details to be found in the bottomless interstices of any such attempted systematisation: those existential particulars and phenomenological niceties loudly proclaimed – from one direction, by Kierkegaard, and from quite another, by Levinas – as being wholly irreducible.

– *After a moment or two of fairly thoughtful silence, the Man in the Purple Jacket – his nose, at this point, a bloated drop of burst capillaries – decides to speak: "We are free to choose. God cannot foresee let alone condone that choice." Harry immediately answers: "Some people would say that the very ability to choose on our part impugns God's power." "What could be more powerful than creating a totally free being?"*

– As described by some of the latest philosophical authors on the tail end of the phenomenological movement (especially Levinas), the Other overspills or crashes over his (or her) plastic form, like an ocean wave. This overspill is excessive glory; the infinite. *Totality and Infinity* brings into discussion this type of 'expressive-shortfall' associated with capturing knowledge of this other subjectivity. But *Totality and Infinity* refers to it as a 'surplus' on the part of the Other rather than a lack inherent in epistemological endeavours: for example, in the many references to the 'surplus of the epiphany of the Other'. Yet our inability, as a subject of experience, to take up – or break through to – this *surplus* of the Other, effectively means that the Other cannot be wholly equated with his expressions in the thought of Levinas. Consequently, there is always more to see, a surplus, always more to say, always more to acknowledge. We never see enough of him (our 'expressive-shortfall'). Expression *testifies* to the existence of an Other – it pinpoints his existence and whereabouts – but does not disclose him *exhaustively*. The stranger who unexpectedly intrudes upon us from the heights also has a somewhat unilluminated inner life in the depths. This deficit of uptake (the 'slack of knowledge', Cavell calls it) *perhaps* returns us to an equation of *unpredictability, incompleteness* and *transcendence…* and ultimately the Other drifts away from his own face.

– Unanticipatable Alterity. We borrow this term from E. Levinas. But doesn't the term seem to reduce transcendence to unpredictability? A trauma deadened by a certain pretence at knowledge?

– *Listen, in secret, to the sound of the steps of the woman two rooms away, two countries away. She's green-eyed and voluntarily blonde. Transference and projection provide the results that knowledge typically claims. I catch a snatch of her telephone conversation. I hear, for example, that: "He came away without a single scratch on him."* I drift away from her, losing interest, slowly.

– Both the Kantian *sublime* and the Levinasian *expressive body* can be said to be *in excess* of the saturation point of subjective human perception – because both are linked, at least at times, to inaccessible ontological depths which aren't amenable to a full phenomenal recuperation. The Schopenhauerian expressive body, on the other hand (like that described by Stanley Cavell), is wholly open to perception. (But isn't it permissible to say that it is yet *in excess* of the saturation point of subjective *conception*?) All three, nonetheless, enshrine a route to morality (in the case of the Kantian sublime, aesthetic and ethics are bridged by the curious emotion of 'respect').

– Man is a coward in the face of gentle perfection. (That we do, in point of fact, accept the evaluation of the Other in this regard, Sartre suggests (with some insidiously persuasive examples), thus explains the phenomena of shame. Not only in sympathy but also in shame do I recognize and accept the Other, a point that Levinas, too, makes in *Totality and Infinity*.)

– *You* couldn't hold on to what you had once found inside you.

– To stimulate (even to accelerate) what Nietzsche takes to be the now practically inevitable long historical process of the (*specifically European*) process of 'nihilism', he provides Europe with a highly polemical form of moral philosophising ("genealogy") that aims primarily to deprecate and ultimately replace all the ethical conclusions that not only Christian ethics but also such contemporary intellectual ethical undertakings as utilitarianism and Schopenhauer's twin projects of rationalist monism and empiricist sentimentalism – intersecting in his 'rational intuitionism'– might be taken to entail. Nietzsche uncompromisingly brushed aside the idea of an atheistic morality as nothing but the philosophical remnants of a now theologically meaningless taboo (there can surely be no scholarly illusions about this now). Nietzsche, unconstrained by the limits of the moral imagination (although much Nietzschean scholarship has yet to digest this point), dismissed the word "evil" as a snarl. Nietzsche's philosophical development – one cannot, to repeat, permit the least ambiguity about this – culminated in the position of him wanting to unsparingly obsolesce what we know as morality. This tendency had its germs right back in the very beginnings of his history of publication. Disregarding the uncharacteristic writings of his period of positivism (I am thinking mainly of *Human, all too human*), right from *The Birth of Tragedy from the Spirit of Music* onwards, in fact, Nietzsche bit down hard on any moralizing tone that he detected in an author. Yet the scholarly commentator's basic gag-reflex on approaching Nietzsche's project of genealogy still remains one of immediately deeming it only a part of an unfinished and far more palatable text – or only a critique of *one specific type* of morality – or only a criticism of *one* conception of morality... *The great innovators change nothing.*

– That infinite black spaces so terrified Pascal indicates that his instincts were in the right place. Any adequate attempt to sublime them into moral entities is no longer even seriously attempted. (Kant circuitously tried to do so *via* the feeling of 'respect' and it is true that certain contemporary physicists occasionally lapse into something not entirely unlike a half-hearted morally affirmative delight, although they prefer the allegedly neutral term 'wonder' to describe their acquiescent bliss.) But black spaces still claw their way toward us. One menacing way in which they have touched us is through recent meditations on the implications of Enrico Fermi's "paradox" concerning the absence of xenocivilisations. But what of the equally infinite vastnesses of the inner tracts? I do not mean here just the infinite silences of the microscopic depths suggested by Zeno of Elea, nor do I mean the vast digestive tracts of gastro-nomic interest to Feuerbach and, to a lesser extent, Nietzsche. (Diet and gastronomy had been an overt issue in the European thought of their day thanks to the "medical materialism" of Jacob Moleschott.) Rather, I mean to refer to the silence *this* side of space: the silence of the human soul. From the point of view of the linguistic breakdown of phenomenological philosophy as it emerges in the work of Derrida in particular, the 'deconstruction' of the soul consists in a patient demonstration that the postulation of a silent and already unified self, hidden away in some recess beyond the reach of language, would be vulnerable to the suspicion that such a figure of muteness would be nothing other than – as Freud had previously hinted at in *On the Interpretation of Dreams* – a symbol of death itself. Total silence; full death: both inaccessible to the living subject *as* functioning living subject. In a harsh violation of scholarly good sense, allow me here a personal disclosure. The following feature of a repeated dream (or dreams) has given me some trouble since the acknowledged emergence of a certain disease within me (the dream goes back seven years): in this or that dream situation in which I find myself, I try but *I still cannot speak*. I gag, I stutter, I am mute, I'm beyond words… But I know that I ought to be reproached: both for being too articulate about my own muteness and for conflating muteness with stuttering.

– The Fichtean version of the subjective idealist – bogeyman solipsist – unknowingly sabotages his own position whenever he tries to articulate it. The solipsist is forever confined by his inability to speak a single – *comprehensible* – word. Such a conclusion follows immediately from even the briefest consideration of Wittgenstein's fragmentary remarks on the idea of a private language. But the same conclusion can also be reached by entirely different philosophic paths. For example: we could reach an equivalent conclusion by an appreciative reading of Heidegger's work on language and even more so Derrida's, which, at least in its earlier phase, consisted mostly of critically close ('double') readings of other philosophical texts on the topics of, precisely, subjectivity and language. Silence – like the ocean – is all surface and all depth.

– Abraham showed nothing, he expressed nothing, said nothing after the acceptance of his commandment. He let out neither a stifled peep nor a suppressed wince (purely verbal evocations of his inner self are, if not actually unnecessary, then at least only supplemental).

– As various philosophers have competently shown (and shown in a variety of ways), Others are necessary for a fully moral life. Yet what allows the Kierkegaardian figuring of Biblical characters such as Abraham in terms of their social sequestration was not at all an overturning of, say, Feuerbachian findings concerning the moral reproof of scepticism existing solely on the basis of the *previously assumed existence* of conspecifics to potentially rectify and at least stand guarantee for our moral judgments but, rather, an acceptance, on Kierkegaard's part, of the gentle pertinence of conspecifics to morality followed by the prospect of an ultimate abandonment or potential sacrifice of morality itself. Kierkegaard thus coupled morality as Hegelian *Sittlichkeit* with *a potentially necessary suspension of the whole social-moral dynamic*. If this still remains an intuitively less disconcerting abandonment of the ethical than was that of Nietzsche, it is no doubt because Nietzsche urged, not the odd individual, but history itself – or at least an entire class of men within history – to set aside morality. Nietzsche deals with an entire people, whereas Kierkegaard takes people on a case-by-case basis. *God has no crowd before Him.*

– *Blue sky: black sun; the infinite emptiness of the universe, the royal surface of the sea. "You get used to everything, in the end. Man's capacity for change outlasts change", thought Harry as, in a moment of blue calm, he looked through the kitchen window and up at the unlimited sky. He touched the window and then touched his chin; which was a lot colder than he had expected.*

– We look upon artworks but we look *into* the glassy-eyed gaze of another subjectivity. Perhaps it is permissible to say that these are two parallel but epistemologically incommensurable zones. We may also want to promote the idea that these realms only ever *tend* toward an ultimate convergence; that these realms only ever asymptotically approach a distance of zero. In Jean-Paul Sartre's phenomenological vocabulary, this unbreachable polarity is captured in the strict divide between the world of the For-Itself and that of the In-Itself. (The "For-Itself" (or *pour-soi*): is the world of the Other subject.) What is at play here is clearly not (not just) the always enigmatic appeal of structure but, mainly, the direct appeal of people in themselves: the call, not of Being, but of people. Unless, perchance, the call of Being is straightaway conceived of as the call of an Infinite Subject, as explicitly occurs in Catholic existentialism. (This is probably the place where Gabriel Marcel proves his importance.)

– There is something almost Godlike about those who bestow upon themselves their very own names in adulthood. They are their own predecessors; they survive their own rebirth.

– The Other – do not have any remaining illusions about her on *this* point – is unannounced; she impinges on your feelings. She is undemonstrated, impertinent and inexpedient. She is imploring, unexpected, insatiable and always in the right. ("Insatiable": if we believe Levinas, then already in this exigency emerges the idea of the Infinite. The infinite is produced in the encounter.) Her ceaseless petitions ensnare you. Every unantici-pated interruption by the other is intrusive, if not actually in every case irritating. You *feel* her unprepossessing impress. You're already a hostage. A life without any such moral molestation as this, on the other hand, is a monstrous and selfish fantasy.

– From the initial conditions of our spatial proximity and the mode of fleshy incarnation that clothes and expresses our metaphysical situation, there further emerges the exigency of responsibility. The infinite is this exigency. As Levinas sees it, in even thinking of you, I am generating the Infinite.

– Expression is the content that we thought had eluded us. Expression is the consent that we thought had always been denied us.

– We are tempted to say that the swell and trickle of vital feelings such as sympathy is prompted by exteriority but is drawn from *inner* sources. The determination of an inner origin remains the case even if Schopenhauer, a maverick Idealist metaphysician (with residual sentimentalist commitments), more or less innocently manipulated the description of his experience of sympathy to make it accord with an elaborate system of metaphysical monism, from time to time suggesting that sympathy, that moral keystone of the Scottish empiricists was, in reality, a "mystical experience" connecting us with the ontological monistic "all": the Outside, "the One" in which we were all identical. Schopenhauer thus definitively breaks with the entire tradition of the Scottish sentimentalists when he ascribes to sympathy (through the aforementioned doctored phenomenology) this darkly metaphysical dimension. Subsequently, Nietzsche had notorious misgivings about the importance ascribed to the sympathetic emotions, not only by Schopenhauer but howsoever such emotions were theoretically underpinned by individual philosophers. Against Nietzsche, one may still intuitively feel that to doubt one's own sympathy is actually to deny one's true character; perhaps even to doubt (a part of) one's essence.

– *Schopenhauerian Nothingness* is ultimately summoned by *The World as Will and Representation* as an inviting absence entered only by withdrawing our will entirely from the world; an operation of detachment that basically involves the subject slowly decorporealizing himself. (Schopenhauer's approach to *Nirvana* has certain obvious points in common with Heideggerean *Gelassenheit*.) The withdrawn and isolated Schopenhauerian subject consequently forgets all the phenomena – in the Kantian sense – of this world, or, at any rate, forgets the sense of all the phenomena of this world, including the sense or meaning of the ephemeral experience of suffering, a process which appears to dangerously include – though Schopenhauer does not address this issue himself – forgetting (hence neglecting) the suffering of others.

– Is it not permissible to say that, in a social setting, there is no such thing as "harmless inattention"?

– Whim or caprice is a decision destitute of any appeal to – or promise of (let alone guarantee of) support from – intersubjectivity. The ethical deficiencies of such an isolation of focus on subjective feeling (as they are found in Shaftsbury, for example) eventually lead us to such *corrective* counter-isolationist philosophical phenomena as the Impartial Spectator of the Enlightenment (a highlight of Adam Smith's moral philosophy), the *Sittlichkeit* of the Hegelian system, the Wittgensteinian language of men in their everyday activities and, of course, to Feuerbach's philosophically indispensable anti-Hegelian postulate: 'the species' (Feuerbach cherished the epistemological gesture of opening up the self to correction by the species). Feuerbach – and here the analysis of his work by Marxists such as Althusser comes to mind – competently springs Hegelian *Geist* from its privileged metaphysical position and replaces the Absoluteness of the Hegelian Idea with the absoluteness of Man (the species). Considering such frameworks of the moral Universal as these (Impartial Spectator, *Sittlichkeit*, the Species), in juxtaposition with the residually empirical element of, say, Schopenhauerian philosophy, it looks *primae facie* as though

Schopenhauer didn't see that a morality cannot both validly exist and yet be dangerously vulnerable to persistent charges of being potentially haphazard. Kierkegaard's formal particularity is entirely different. Kierkegaard leaves the frameworks of universal morality entirely untouched. The Kierkegaardian fixation upon the self and Protestant interior reality at the expence of the community left him theoretically open to charges of his choices of action being capricious, mad, wrong or whimsical. (The instant of decision, Kierkegaard openly admitted, *was* madness.) Kierkegaard courted these charges as an act of religious piety. A piety that not only protested against the contemporary church but that could not, on principle, accept any church.

– If moral knowing is first person plural, religious knowing, as Kierkegaard presupposes from the outset, is always singular.

– The Levinasian Other grants us something of himself but *even he* is not quite satisfied with the impression he makes on us. The expression of the face isn't a wholly transparent access to the Other for Levinas but is rather only a kind of *asymptotic* contact. The realm of human subjectivity is still seen as something of a closed realm: an argument could be concocted (perhaps by a fervent neo-Leibnitzean) that this realm is a mutually inaccessible set of closed dominions. But the trauma of the mutual creates an exterior impulsion received as an overwhelming shock wave that's to be accepted – or acknowledged, or respected – rather than known.

– *A Note for the Grossly Inattentive*: What we actually see is recalcitrant to full epistemological uptake but is nonetheless still anchored in expressive reality. We are overwrought by the alterity that is found in sensuous exteriority (what Levinas has beautifully called the surplus of epiphany) and by the constantly

renewed – never able to be fully discharged (Infinite) – obligations of this impress. We are implicitly forced to acknowledge, *in
situ* and in practice, the always ethically charged existence of the
Other – but as to the exact form that this particular force and this
particular acknowledgement should take: here, one has to admit,
we often – but not always – seem to be operating entirely without
instructions. One might choose to claim that precisely here,
entering the zone of human goodness, we are living under our
own supervision – were it not for the bewildering peril of
possible caprice. Something else emerges as being clear here: not
only are we not moral isolationists (in the sense that Shaftsbury
and Sartre were) but neither are we "moral volunteers": we have
not elected to be here in a specifically ethical capacity. (We
actually impinge here on three entirely separate philosophical
themes: firstly, the phenomenological doctrine of 'throwness' –
Heideggerean 'Geworfenheit', Sartrean 'facticity', Levinasian
'lateness' – as well as, secondly, the notion of moral luck and,
thirdly and finally, Levinasian ideas of being a moral detainee or
'hostage'.)

– Our pleasures, pains and passions are just as private as our
faces. He who knows how to read a face does not need to
decipher a diary.

– Although you can talk to yourself, you can't converse. To enter
into a conversation is itself a *form* of acknowledgement, in that it
is already to tacitly enter into alliance with (or adherence to)
certain pre-existing social conventions – aspiring to the ideal
speech situation (Habermas); entering a certain language game
associated with a given form of life (Wittgenstein); opening
oneself up to correction by other members of our species
(Feuerbach); taking up the framework of specific conventions
that implicitly govern the use of certain words said *by*
(sometimes, specifically assigned) individuals (J. L. Austin).

Remember that those who found that they could not follow the convention of keeping up with the logical progress of a Socratic dialogue (whether through lack of education or dim wittedness or sloth or inattention or illogicality or over-exuberance) had to physically or spiritually leave the dialogue – and sometimes they physically left the scene of instruction with quite risible 'justifications'.

– One doesn't need a pseudonym in private.

– The idea that something important and essential remains secreted – *or should remain secreted* – concealed, unnoticeable, hidden in the deeper reaches of the human spirit was entertained – and it probably can be pushed no further than it was – by Kierkegaard. (It would be a distraction to discuss here that there are complications incurred in our reading of Kierkegaard to the degree that we recognize that certain of his works are pseudonymous – i.e. that they belong to what he liked to call *the series of the left hand*.) Kierkegaard's *The Concluding Unscientific Postscript* straightforwardly tells us that: 'Inwardness is untrue in direct proportion to the ready availability of external expressions in countenance and bearing'[13]. The object of this passage is to establish that the inner truth and integrity of your subjectivity is manipulated and compromised by your lazy or wilful or conformist adoption of socially available gestures as well as by the adoption of iterable words. (Your own interiority isn't inscribed within what you presumptuously tend to call "your" language.) Similar themes are developed in other of Kierkegaard's later works: *The Sickness Unto Death*, for instance, tells us that the more spiritual that 'inner despair' becomes then 'the more attention it pays to neutralizing the externalities, making them as insignificant and inconsequential as possible'[14]. (But just how far *is it* possible?) The philosophical picture emerging from such Kierkegaardian passages is that the essential dramatic externalities or standard socially available external expressions and words can (and from a purely spiritual viewpoint, should), be hidden or discarded by the inner self, to the extent that this is possible, at any rate. The soul or spirit should hold, more purely, to a *silent interior standard.* Kierkegaard's picking up on the importance of this *suppression of expression* allowed him all of his efforts related to the desire to release the invisible majesty of bourgeois heroes.

– *Phillipa picks up the frying pan: "Do you want me to do you an egg?" "What are you, a bloody chicken?" Phillipa looks at her seated visitors and draws an expression of pantomimed disapproval, her green eyes widening. The truth is: she loves this kind of routine. Harry concludes with a flourish:"Lay off the eggs, ladies, they bung you right up."*

– The extent to which you take the word "conscientiousness" to be beautiful is a measure of your capacity for religion. No ordinary measure.

– *Harry picks up the mobile: "Hello. Hello. Can you hear me? Can you hear me?" There is a pause. He ends the call as abruptly as it started. "Wrong number. Wrong number!" Harry intones. He then turns around and, with a transient sense of foreboding, declares to the room: "Wrong number… I don't like the sound of that."*

– Representational isomorphism is prohibited in Kantian metaphysics by the absence of a principle of noumenal (hence 'real') individuation. As this ultimately Schopenhauerian point may also be put: logics of noumenal delineation – such as the Kantian line of thought tacitly contained in the belief in separable postulates of practical reason: e.g. God, souls – are flawed from the very outset. Such a principle follows immediately from Schopenhauer's coupling of the ultimately Lockean notion that space and time are the way that we differentiate objects with the Kantian declaration that space and time are absent from the noumenal realm, the world of the Thing-in-Itself. Hence the merest Kantian *suggestion* of the noumenal and phenomenal co-occurance of separate selves, for example, must be taken to be philosophically problematic.

– That aggresively atheistic post-Kantian strand of philosophy running from Schopenhauer through Nietzsche and beyond is – certainly when contrasted with the Hegelian reception of Kant – most disarming when it displays its totally unpretentious inability to accommodate most of its own conclusions. Moments of human kindness and geniune sympathy, for instance, are crucial for Schopenhauer's view of the world and its meaning. However, *stricto sensu* they're nothing but inexplicable anomalies in terms of the workings of his ontology. For Schopenhauer is at bottom a monist who posits an ontologically ultimate selfish will – but one who, nonetheless, still values ethical and self-sacrificing acts. How? What principle can possibly account for or motivate these charitable acts? (Bizarrely, the philosophy of Levinas converges with that of Schopenhauer around just this set of problems.) Somewhat unpredictably, Schopenhauer at this point allows key charitable moments of human kindness and sympathy to fall out of the realm of philosophical explanation altogther. With some subtlety, he slides these charitable moments into the separate religious sphere of 'grace' and from such a borderline-theological position, it is scarcely a leap of any conceptual distance to the similar position eventually adopted by Levinas, according to whom ontology is, once again, utterly egoistic in nature but that moments of uncalculated and unreciprocal 'holiness' or 'sanctity', strictly incommensurable with an ontological view of the world, nevertheless do happen. (How often?)

– *The infinitely terrible sky stretches out: Harry had, before going up to a flat rooftop with the others, vastly underestimated the force of the new c.d.e walloping in to the blood of the brain and had to pretend to be distracted away from polite conversation by high-minded thoughts and not, as was in fact the case, by raw exo-interior experience. The c.d.e itself reached out beyond personality and simply gleamed, like the stars themselves.*

– Perhaps it is *pain* that juts out from the immanence of the world – unless it is pain that drags us more densely into its sod.

– Those, such as Heidegger and Tolstoy, who appear to find it of most existential importance to face their own death are to be placed against those generally lesser known writers who find the death of other people more significant, moving and imperative (in this respect, the novels of Saul Bellow and the philosophy of Gabriel Marcel are especially instructive). But then there are bystanders. Bystanders as such may not necessarily be negligent: they might be present for you in your loss, for example – but they cannot comfort you. They remain awkwardly present, for the moment effectively – and literally – repressing a death that will eventually return to undo them.

– 'Human reality' – a mistranslation I adopt here advisedly – as construed in *Being and Time* would seem to be concretised by Heidegger as a *very capable subject* – *Dasein* is *competent by definition* – decisively exercising his capabilities against the bracing acknowledgement of death as the ultimate human horizon of all choices, projects and accomplishments. One cannot easily imagine a hapless *Dasein*. *Dasein* is reliable. It is through the very *reliability* of humanity, we are much later told by Heidegger, that man hears the call of the earth.

– It can be obvious at a glance that the gaze of an Other excites and addresses our pity or, at any rate, incites a response of some sort. And a noncommittal response is still a response (and not the postponement or the absence of a response, as you might initially think).

– *"You are Here"*: We are irrevocably committed to an attachment, from which we simply cannot withdraw (without denying or abandoning our commitment and claim to goodness): we are not monsters. Moreover (bordering, here, on the theme of 'throwness'), we are there (here) *de facto* and so consequently *de jure*. This is the *a priori* structure of social responsibility (that of being an unransomed 'hostage'). Such 'election' devolves from – or it *structures* – intersubjective interactions as such, which will always be a matter of contingency in the particular. (The Other who appoints me as elect will just be the first one who happens to come along.)

– Each one is chosen. (I believe it was Bruno Bauer who said: "Privilege remains privilege even when it extends to all".)

– The grandiose Hegelian project of systematically developing an ontologically inflated articulation of human historical self-realization as the incarnate life of 'spirit' or '*Geist*' was soon whittled down by those young Hegelians who told the story of the alienation of our 'species being' – where man first found the principle of his alienation in God. This residue of *Geist* was further pared down in the subsequent 'historical materialism' of Marx, where man found the principle of his alienation in the commodification of the process of a *specifically human labour*. Max Stirner refashioned Feuerbachian dialectical entanglements over the 'alienation' of 'species being' into a far more domestic concern: the life of the paltry ego. The poor little I contesting the abstraction of the species, signals, in the case of Stirner, a political transfer from the left to the anarchic libertarian right. Nietzsche, whatever his historical debts to Stirner, is notable for taking a theoretical leap not *over* Stirner's Egoism, however, but *under* it – i.e. for shifting his attention *directly to the body underlying and determining the character of the ego.* (Today, Nietzsche would centre all of his scholarly attention – with a maximum level of controversy – on the genes. But because Nietzsche unflinchingly undermined the cherished ideals of a *previous age* he is thus misguidedly adored by our own.)

– There are certain people who are always running to you at full pelt – but only because they're running away from themselves. There can be no final destination, in this world, for them. (*This is nothing but a sketch of the noise that is made when the time-shields of two human pathologies clash.*)

– For the most part, it is love that drives us into solitude.

– Levinas' most overpowering formula, which may be inadequately summarised here as the demand: 'You should come to a halt before the moral impress of the body' appears *primae facie* to be the very invocation of form. As such, it would be to some degree compromised by the fact that human expression is itself the 'break up' of form (Levinas repeatedly states this). A physically detectable expression is, therefore, not itself physical, which is exactly why it is also summarised as the *breakthrough* or *break up* of form. It is not the anatomical human features that are crucial to the face, then, so much as it is *the play* of those features, the spirit animating them. What matters is not so much the iris as the gaze.

– The Other, either willingly or unwillingly, makes her obtrusive impression simply – she votes with her feet; stakes her ethical case with her movements and her expression. Yet it is perhaps true that she comes into focus as that which cannot be fully *conceptually comprehended.* Faces are too fine grained for the concept. In terms strictly belonging to Schopenhauer's philosophy: the face can only be felt. (There is non-conceptual content in our experience of particular faces.) In terms belonging to Wittgenstein's philosophy: measurements can't catch the expression of a face. In terms of reference that belong to Marcel Proust: our knowledge of faces is not mathematical.

– 04:44 A.M. and it dawns on you: it *was* something like the obliterating power of opium when you thought it was a kind of absolution that you'd gathered from the arms of empty time. In the darkness, I think of Hölderlin, who (mistakenly) equated God with time, the transport of empty time.

– Regina Olsen stared out of the window, as silent as the biblical Sarah – who watched them go together, down into the valley.

– If you don't possess any feelings of responsibility whatsoever and you can't even find inside yourself a trickle of sympathy – then you can simply face down the Other, plain and simple. Cut them loose. You'll have to harbour the social cost of being a considered monster (and you'll deserve it) but if you can survive incurring such ostracism (what's some shunning between friends?) you will be able to face her or him down, as bold as brass. Nietzsche believes in something not dissimilar to this.

– *Good*: Nietzsche earnestly wanted a cultural goal right from the beginning. For although *The Birth of Tragedy* ostensibly treated the scholarly topic of Ancient Attic theatre, its driving impulse was really Nietzsche's clear recognition of the *cultural needs* of the present: the avoidance of sliding into nihilism. But Nietzsche says nothing at all substantive about one of his key mature goals, the *Übermensch*, leading to persuasive suspicions that it only has any substance as an empty and redemptive symbol of an existential goal: a tawdry consolation for humanity, some might think. The *Übermensch* is clearly a form our species must aim at – but nowhere is it depicted and developed by Nietzsche with much more depth than this.

– *Harry and Phillipa sat in their reasonably priced kitchen. This was around forty or so minutes after the man in the purple jacket had left. They were emotionally and physically drained. Some vague misgivings once entertained by the couple about the man in purple had, by now, sclerotised into hardened moral judgments. It was Harry who began to speak: "Do you see any evil in him, Phillipa?" "Well, "Evil" is a very big word, Harry." "No, Phillipa, it isn't. It really isn't."*

– Any system that perfectly accounts for the fragment must thereby begin to destroy it.

– Extreme clarity can be another form of distortion.

– Extreme pain can, in the work of some writers, appear as a tense splicing of social *dependence* with an utter epistemological *isolation*. One senses this occasionally in Wittgenstein and, more obscurely, in E. M. Cioran. Hegel's surprising thought (articulated in the *Philosophy of History*) was that it is actually in pain that man realizes his subjectivity. But the contrary is clearly true, at least at the extremes: in the most painful suffering, man *loses* his independent subjectivity. The pain undoes him and at this point, he enters a realm of *infantile dependence* upon others. Such dependence was at one time almost a commonplace: another example of a social necessity becoming a cultural taboo.

– "But pain can be *harnessed, somehow* overcome" I take this optimistic – and, therefore, perhaps necessary – piece of advice to be one of the key idealistic presuppositions of a whole range of self-bolstering ideas important to the mature Nietzsche and also increasingly significant to contemporary popular culture. Irrespective of – and probably connected to – their culturally fashionable status, however, almost all of these notions are empirically questionable.

– Nietzsche's peopling of *On the Genealogy of Morality* with such an oddly entertaining cast of human types is both more complex and more assured than it appears to be at second glance. The song of the poet, the chant of the priest, the cry of the warrior: all audible to the ear of the philologist. And the master, by his actions, accomplishes what the poet, by his words, cannot. But the insightful poet detects the Achilles' heel of the master: "With every mighty step the hero takes we hear the dull echo of death"[15] – the hero's own. The master turns to the poet for a form of immortality but certain poets step out of line and speak in the new name of *religion*: 'I have seen penitents of the spirit appearing: they grew out of the poets' Nietzsche says in a section of *Thus Spoke Zarathustra* (entitled *Of Poets*). Thus – Nietzsche's argument runs – begins the entire degeneration of Western civilization.

– It is a central practical commitment of *Being and Time* that *Dasein* resolutely orient himself toward death, step by step ignoring the real possibilities – whatever Heidegger says about methodologically screening off a decision about them – of religion, as well as ignoring certain existential difficulties posed by technological advances (internal advances of the forces of production that change the essence of the producer), such as, especially, extropianism. Nothing must divert Heidegger from facing death and the phenomenological horizon of the post-phenomenological subject must, it follows, be deliberatedly and pre-emptively closed on all sides of truth – whether these specific truths be either scientific or religious in their nature.

– It always seems a little too early to be reconciled to the future.

– Nothing disrupts like silence.

– *Phillipa pressed her gloved hand against the glass and breathed an ambitious cloud of opaque mist onto the cold, unfrosted window. Her Russian hat, maternally inherited, with its teddy bear aspect, added an alarming touch of panache to that obscurely instinctive gesture. Harry delightedly let her in to the warm.*

– "I caught my colours in the dreadful mourning." "How are we to understand this?" "In a totally fictitious sense." She grants this freedom; she is not at my disposal, she gives me time.

– In the *Philosophical Investigations* but also, for example, the *Last Writings on the Philosophy of Psychology*, Wittgenstein appears to suggest that the Other is implicitly perceived as an essentially bodily *expressive linguistic corrector* – in some cases (answering or not answering to his name, for example) even a clever dog could adequately function in this role. Levinas might, to a limited extent, identify with such a characterization: the Other might well be said to be a corporeal expressive enigma in Levinas (though not so much a 'corrector'); still (almost) as ineliminably expressive but heading inexorably – and, typically, despite its own most profound wishes for a protracted existence – toward the desperately sad state of total inexpression. Inexpression is objectivity and when inexpression – objectivity – is being pondered as a destination for people – people we may know and even love – then the process being described can only be heart-breaking. It is pure presence at hand, objectivity, that is wholly expressionless: "Someone who dies: a face that becomes a mask. The expression disappears."[16] The Other is stifled in a variety of ways by a variety of illnesses but he or she is stilled by death. The conversation simply cannot continue. Since the face no longer remains a face in death it obviously isn't the notion of the literal anatomical face that is crucial for Levinas when invoking the notion of the *visage*, it is the face as *expressing*, the face *as expressive face*. Inexpression may also be a living way in which, whilst in very severe pain, a man fails to realize, express and accomplish his personal subjectivity, the severity of pain in this case is actually *blocking* the fullness of his expressive life rather than ending it outright. Illness and suffering can, in such ways, intervene and disrupt the otherwise crucial relationship between subjectivity and expression, blocking the supply of subjectivity and circling downwards toward the impersonal, the trauma of radically unknown horror.

– The singular event of an encounter with the other is, time and time again, characterized by Levinas as trauma: a *discontinuous shock felt at the site of a deep unknowing*. This is an intimate contact that fissures the general hard-heartedness that presumably remains intact in the face of that other more impersonal kind of trauma: horror of the impersonal unknown.

– Trauma is, simultaneously, recovery.

– *Keith is overstepping the bounds of the acceptable. He has deliberately remained unshaven for several weeks. He now places his feet in the preposterously outmoded shoes that he reserves for such occasions; he quickly glances in the mirror, dons his lilac jacket and readies himself for the transformation that quickly occurs, in the narrow space of the hallway, during the journey between the lounge and the front door. We are outside, standing on the path next to the lawn of the front garden. Suddenly, there is movement. The latch clicks, the door opens, Keith walks forward. The man in the purple jacket has arrived.*

Endnotes

1. E. Levinas, *Totality and Infinity* (Pittsburgh: Duquesne University Press, 1969), 75.
2. Levinas, *Totality and Infinity*, 181.
3. L. Feuerbach, *The Essence of Christianity* (New York: Prometheus, 1989), 140.
4. Levinas, *Totality and Infinity*, 121. In modern philosophical thought, it is doubtless Heidegger in *Being and Time* (Oxford: Blackwell, 1995) as well as Wittgenstein in the *Philosophical Investigations* (Oxford: Blackwell, 1998) who have, independently of one another, best typified a relatively new concentration on how the subject primarily relates to the world: human practical activity. If such a conception can be seen to raise inescapable questions about the customary epistemological analysis of the subject relating to the world primarily in terms of *knowledge*, it becomes possible to then further argue for the displacement of the central role earlier granted to epistemology (particularly on the question of Others) by highlighting the *ethical importance* of human relations. Variations of a solution – or reproof – of scepticism along such moral lines are undertaken in both the Heideggerean and the Wittgensteinian traditions: more specifically, both by Levinas in *Totality and Infinity* and by Stanley Cavell in *The Claim of Reason: Wittgenstein, Skepticism, Morality and Tragedy* (Cambridge: Harvard University Press, 1982), where, in both cases, moral acceptance is taken to recoup what overflows epistemology. A synthesized appreciation of the results of both dispensations is argued for in Søren Overgaard's *Wittgenstein and Other Minds: Rethinking Subjectivity and Intersubjectivity with Wittgenstein, Levinas and Husserl* (Routledge: London, 2007).
5. A. Schopenhauer, *The World as Will and Representation*, Vol. I

(New York: Dover, 1962), 100.

6. G. W. F. Hegel, *The Philosophy of History* (New York: Dover, 1956), 68.

7. E. Levinas, *Time and the Other* (Pittsburgh: Duquesne University Press, 1987), 90.

8. L. Wittgenstein, *Last Writings on the Philosophy of Psychology*, Vol. 2 (Oxford: Blackwell, 2009), 41; see also the fragment contained in his *Last Writings on the Philosophy of Psychology*, Vol. 1 (Oxford: Blackwell, 1982), §10.

9. Schopenhauer, *The World as Will and Representation*, Vol. II (New York: Dover, 1969), 326.

10. F. Nietzsche, *Writings From the Late Notebooks* (Cambridge: Cambridge University Press, 2003), 220. For a parallel text, see Nietzsche's *Will to Power* (New York: Vintage: 1968), §303: 'Man, a little eccentric species of animal which – fortunately – has had its day; all on earth a mere moment, an incident, an exception without consequences...'.

11. The satirical interpretation of part IV of *Thus Spoke Zarathustra* was introduced by Walter Brogan in 'Zarathustra: The tragic figure of the last philosopher' in Miguel de Beistegui and Simon Sparks (eds.) *Philosophy and Tragedy* (London: Routledge, 2000), 152-166 and then developed in a close scholarly reading by Paul S. Loeb in *The Death of Nietzsche's Zarathustra* (Cambridge: Cambridge University Press, 2010).

12. Schopenhauer, *The World as Will and Representation*, Vol. I, 196.

13. S. Kierkegaard, *Concluding Unscientific Postscript to Philosophical Fragments* (Princeton: Princeton University Press, 1992), 236.

14. S. Kierkegaard, *The Sickness Unto Death* (Princeton: Princeton University Press, 1992), 73.

15. Nietzsche, "Richard Wagner in Bayreuth" in *Untimely Meditations* (Cambridge: Cambridge University Press, 1983),

pp. 195-254, 224.

16. Levinas, *God, Death and Time* (Stanford: Stanford University Press, 1991), 12.

BOOKS

Iff Books is interested in ideas and reasoning. It publishes material on science, philosophy and law. Iff Books aims to work with authors and titles that augment our understanding of the human condition, society and civilisation, and the world or universe in which we live.